AGAINST
the
Wind

How women can be their authentic
selves in male-dominated professions

JENNIFER WITTWER, CSM

First published in 2020 by Jennifer Wittwer

© Jennifer Wittwer 2020

The moral rights of the author have been asserted

A catalogue entry for this book is available from the National Library of Australia.

ISBN: 978-1-925921-56-4

Printed in Australia by McPherson's Printing
Project management and text design by Michael Hanrahan Publishing
Cover design by Peter Reardon
Photograph of Jennifer on front cover courtesy of Bradley Cummings, APP

Disclaimer

Contents

*For my daughters Taylah and Chaeleigh:
forever my inspiration and my muses.*

*And for all the women in my life,
particularly those dedicated to the
service of their country.*

About the author

Jennifer provides specialised services to help women and organisations address the challenges of their participation and representation in male-dominated workplaces. She also uses her unique experiences and skills to coach and mentor women looking to fulfil their passions and take new directions in their careers.

In April 2018, Jennifer retired from full-time service in the Australian Defence Force (ADF) as a maritime logistics officer and strategic human resource specialist. She has thirty-eight years' experience in leading people through organisational change and large-scale cultural and workplace reform, and implementing contemporary and niched people-oriented policy strategies and policy solutions. Over the past ten years she has developed and implemented workplace behaviour education programs, and women's leadership, mentoring and network programs and strategies. She has also advised senior ADF leadership on women's representation and participation, and on gender equality and diversity policies and initiatives.

From 2012, Jennifer led the implementation of the United Nations (UN) Women, Peace and Security (WPS) agenda within the ADF and the broader defence and security sector. She has participated in various North Atlantic Treaty Organization (NATO) and UN forums and projects relating to WPS and women's representation in armed forces, and she deployed as the first ADF gender adviser to NATO operations in Afghanistan in 2013. On her return, she was appointed to coordinate the implementation of the Australian Government National Action Plan (NAP) on WPS into ADF operations. In her last ADF role, Jennifer was seconded to UN Women in New York as a policy specialist on peacekeeping and sexual exploitation and abuse.

Since then, Jennifer has contracted to UN Women Ukraine to develop a training framework on gender and WPS for their armed forces, and authored a course on sexual violence in conflict and gender equality in peacekeeping for the Peace Operations Training Institute in the United States. Jennifer is currently contracted to UN Women Jordan to assist with the implementation of the Jordanian NAP on WPS in their defence and security sector over two years.

Jennifer has been recognised with a number of national awards, including the 2010 Australian Centre for Leadership for Women Advancement of Women in the Workplace Award (Bronze), finalist in the 2011 ACT Telstra Business Women's Awards, Conspicuous Service Medal in the 2013 Queen's Birthday Honours List, finalist in the 2014 and 2018 *AFR* 100 Women of Influence, and acknowledgement in the 2016, 2017 and 2018 editions of Who's Who of Australian Women.

In 2018, Jennifer was named the Canberra Women in Business Mentor of the Year and, in 2019, she was a finalist in the Australian Defence Magazine Women in Defence Awards, and the Silver award winner for Most Inspirational Y in the YFactor Awards. She has also been awarded the NATO Afghanistan Medal, Australian Active Service Medal with Clasp ICAT, Afghanistan Medal, Defence Long Service Medal with Fourth Clasp, Australian Defence Medal, UN Medal with Numeral 2, and Returned from Active Service Badge.

Jennifer is a keynote speaker and has written extensively on gender equality, women's participation in the security sector, and women's roles in peace and security efforts. Her work has been featured in the Australian Strategic Policy Institute's *The Strategist*, the US-based *The Strategy Bridge*, US Naval War College 'Proceedings', the Australian Defence Force Journal, the online ANZ Women Thought Leaders Series, Women's Agenda, and various professional journals and blogs. In 2018, Jennifer was published in the inaugural international *Oxford Handbook on Women, Peace and Security*.

Jennifer has a Graduate Certificate in Gender, Peace and Security from Monash University, which she completed in January 2020. She also holds Graduate Diplomas in strategic leadership and resource management, and Graduate Certificates in management studies and administration. Jennifer is undertaking a Master's in International Development from 2020 at University of Canberra. In 2019, Jennifer was appointed a Non-Executive Director to the board of the International Women's Development Agency, and an Ambassador for Women in Business Awards of Australia.

Acknowledgements

In this book, I mention a few people who have had a remarkable impact on me and on my journey. It's important to recognise both the women and men who have influenced, mentored, coached, supported and believed in me, and who gave me the space, trust and freedom to achieve the milestones I did.

Thank you firstly to a few senior military men who believed in me and enabled me to follow my passion: Martin Brooker, a friend and mentor of over 38 years (we trained at the Royal Australian Naval College (RANC) together) who always provided sage advice and wise counsel; a few marvellous bosses (retired), Admirals Davyd Thomas and Trevor Jones, when they were at different times Deputy Chief of Navy, and Air Chief Marshal Mark Binskin, as Chief of the Defence Force; Paul Quinn, retired Royal Navy (RN) Captain; and a couple of Generals, Jody Osterman, United States Marine Corp (USMC), and Gus McLachlan, Australian Army, from my time in Afghanistan. These are all amazing men who supported me and gave me so much opportunity.

Thank you to the inspirational women working on gender in some capacity whom I have come to know: Elizabeth Broderick, previously Australia's Sex Discrimination Commissioner; Julie Mckay, in her capacity as Executive Director UN Women Australia; Paivi Kannisto, head of Peace and Security in UN Women, New York; Avril Henry and Catherine Fox, from their time on the Chief of Defence Force's Gender Equality Advisory Board; Mari Sköre and Marriet Schurmman, the first two NATO Special Representatives for Women, Peace and Security in Brussels; Jacqui True and Katrina Lee-Koo, two of the finest academics I know in the field of gender, peace and security; coaches Amanda Rose, Amanda Cromer, Maureen

Frank, and journalist and gender advocate Virginia Haussegger. There are too many others to name, but I thank all the amazing women working in these areas.

And thank you to a small select group of women I have been mentoring over some years, who continue to allow me to influence and shape their direction and progress in their careers: Trish Dollisson, Kristy Bates, Sarah Brown, Bianca Prain, Belinda Johnson, Amanda Van der Pavard, all from the ADF, and Vasiliki Sartzetaki from the Greek Navy. I'm very proud of the successes and achievements of these wonderful and inspirational women, all of whom I'm sure you'll hear about in time.

Thanks must also go to a small group of girlfriends and my daughter Taylah who took the time to read and critique parts of the manuscript: Julie Mitchell, Kate Boyce-Pointer and Peta Irving.

Thank you to Andrew Griffiths, entrepreneur and business author, whose writing retreat I attended in Bali in July 2019 and who inspired and motivated me to get on and write, to Michael Hanrahan, my publisher, who patiently held my hand through this process, and to Charlotte Duff, my amazing editor who helped finesse and refine the story you will read in the coming chapters.

Thank you to everyone who has supported me along my journey and to those who also believed my story should be told so we can learn from the lessons of the past to create a new future for women.

And lastly, despite the many challenges I faced, I must give thanks to the Royal Australian Navy (RAN). The Navy trained me, gave me educational qualifications and leadership development, shaped and influenced my attributes, skills and values, and, mostly, created an environment in which I met and worked with outstanding women and men in Australia and across the world. Some these challenges may have broken others—and they certainly tested my internal fortitude and 'grit'—but ultimately left me with a spirit and passion for achieving more in, and with, my life.

This book is part of that.

Foreword

The journey for equality for women has been hundreds of years in the making and, at the current rate of change, it may well be another 100 years or more before we have gender equality in terms of women in leadership and pay equity.

Great strides have been made for women in the workplace. This includes women being 'allowed' to work after marriage, being 'allowed' to have their own bank accounts and credit cards, access to paid maternity leave, the ability to work while pregnant, the ability to return to work after childbirth, and an increase in the number of women in leadership roles, women on boards of Australian Stock Exchange–listed companies, and other similar institutions around the world. However, progress is still hampered by unconscious bias, systemic discrimination against women in terms of recruitment, promotion and pay equity, and sexual harassment at work due to patriarchal hierarchies and outdated policies and practices stuck in the 1950s—all while we try to navigate work and living in the next century.

Generational change is driving a re-definition of society standards and workplace expectations due to Generation X (born 1965–1979) and Generation Y (born 1980–1995), who have a different view of loyalty, career, work environment, work–life balance, flexibility and leadership from those generations—namely Baby Boomers (born 1946–1964) and Veterans (born prior to 1946)—who have established the current workplace practices, policies and leadership styles, and now resist change. Today, Generation X and Y women are the most educated in employment history, they have skills, experience and opinions, and they are being frustrated by their lack of progress despite demographics illustrating that they are a serious part of the resources pool. This is why the segment of small businesses being set up by female entrepreneurs is one of the fastest growing in today's economy. And they are successful!

As a nation, we still appear to overlook that, economically, women are a serious part of our workforce and critically important to our future as a nation. Women make up 52 per cent of the population of Australia (46 per cent of the full-time workforce and 75 per cent of the part-time workforce), while 60 per cent of tertiary graduates are now women! And yet women are still paid less than men for doing the same job, will retire with less or no superannuation compared to men, and are more likely to become homeless after the age of 55 than men. We should all be disappointed in these statistics for our mothers, our daughters, our sisters, our granddaughters and our female friends. How can we let this continue? What can and should we do individually and collectively?

Women want advice, support and help in navigating what is still a man's world, despite women's progress in terms of educating themselves for improved lives and financial security. How do women compete fairly in male-dominated professions?

Jennifer's book is a wonderful handbook on how to successfully navigate our male-dominated world; and it is not just professions that are dominated by men, but all three power bases of our global society—politics, big business and religious institutions. Jennifer is not a victim, even though it would be understandable if she chose to be one, given her many challenging and discriminatory experiences. She chose instead to be the master of her own destiny, to learn from each challenge and negative experience, to challenge the status quo and above all to remain true to herself and her passion for helping other women.

This book is a treasure chest of golden nuggets. It is filled with practical advice, check lists and exercises to challenge every woman looking to succeed on her own terms in a world that is dominated by men and the choices they make for women at work. This book sets the scene for how things have been and largely remain for women at work, along with how to work out what you want in your career and life, why and when, and whether it is congruent with your personal values. It is easy to read—I devoured it in a weekend—and, importantly, it is easy to understand and implement. It is a great road map for success, and I'm sure you will find yourself returning to this book again and again. I know I will.

Jennifer shares her difficulties and her triumphs with great dignity, humour and humility. She is passionate, articulate and encouraging. She generously shares her experience, knowledge and ideas with only one objective in mind—to empower women so that they may create meaningful lives and reach their full potential.

Women are still not at the table in equal numbers, we are simply on the table being analysed to determine if we are worthy! And we will never be seen as worthy if we do not step up and speak up, and if we continue to 'be like men', be 'one of the boys', play by their rules and blend in rather than challenge the status quo! We do not want to be treated the same as men, because we are not the same—we are women! We want to be treated fairly, given the same opportunities and pay, and, most of all, to be treated with respect!

I applaud Jennifer for her call to action to all women who care about their careers: 'Be what you can't see. Be the first.' In doing this, you give permission to yourself and to other women to do the same.

My advice to women is don't blend in, don't be beige, no one remembers beige—instead, be purple, be bold, be brave, be determined, be tenacious and keep it real! And remember—you've got this!

Avril Henry
Sydney, November 2019

Preface

Some of the best days of our lives haven't happened yet.

Anne Frank

This book documents the challenges faced by women in traditionally male-dominated professions. But it's so much more than that. Importantly, I explore how women can, using their own power, command their careers in ways that will enable them to achieve their full potential—even if that often means sailing against the wind.

Woven through the book is my own story as a woman officer in the RAN, which took me from being a disempowered and disadvantaged trainee in 1981, to working as an international consultant to the UN in 2018. During the intervening years, I experienced many challenges relating to discrimination, sexual abuse, sexual harassment, intimidation and bullying. Overcoming this adversity led me to opportunities that would eventually allow me to pursue my passion for women's equality and equal rights—for the women of our very proud and professional ADF, as well as the women of armed forces in many other nations.

As you may have already noticed, I've dedicated this book to all the women in my life, not the least my two daughters, Taylah Jessie and Chaeleigh Rae. In 2019, at the time of writing this book, Taylah turned 22 years old, completed her four-year double Bachelor of Arts degree in international studies and political communications at the University of Canberra, and has just landed her first job as an events and communications assistant with a boutique brewery in Canberra. Chaeleigh, at 19 years old, has deferred her double Bachelor of Arts degree in criminology and psychology at the Australian National University and is taking a gap year working as a contracted public servant in a large federal government agency.

Both of these amazing young women are embodying, enjoying and appreciating the freedom of choice available to all women today in studying and working in their chosen fields. I brought them up to believe they could be anything they wanted to be, and I am proud of their achievements and how they are making their way in the world. And it's not just my daughters I see making inroads into male-dominated professions. I see this now all the time with the women I have the immense pleasure and privilege of working with and serving, in my previous roles in the Australian military and now as a consultant, mentor and coach.

Through my work with the Australian Government, the NATO[1] in Brussels and Afghanistan, through to the UN in New York, and other countries around the world, I have seen—and played a part in—some amazing advances in women's participation and representation in armed forces and security agencies. I have held roles focusing on national and international strategic priorities in women's roles in peace and security efforts. Much of my work now, as a consultant, is still focused on these important areas.

The book is a reflection on the male-dominated occupations and workplaces I have experienced while also providing the practical 'how to' strategies I have developed that can help you to overcome the challenges, adversity, complexities, and obstacles that women face throughout their careers. In these situations, we are often told women 'can't be who they can't see'—that is, that navigating male-dominated professions is even more difficult for women if they don't have other women to look to as examples. While I agree with this argument, and the push for more visible women underlying it, I also argue sometimes you can't wait for these role models to appear. So my mantra throughout this book is, in the absence of role models, focus on positioning yourself to *be what you can't see*.

---

1   NATO is an intergovernmental military alliance between 29 North American and European countries.

SAILING WITH AND AGAINST THE WIND

My own journey significantly shaped who I was and how I became who I couldn't see.

I was always destined to join the Australian military. My father, Graham, was a pilot in the Royal Australian Air Force (RAAF), but sadly died in a flying accident at Point Cook, Victoria, on 28 June 1961. My mother, Janne, a clerk in the RAAF, had of course been discharged on marriage in 1959. She had a two-year-old daughter, my sister Louise, and was pregnant with me when Graham passed away.

She was quite a remarkable woman for her time. She had suffered significant adversity in her life (all before she gave birth to me, at the age of 23), yet when my father died she packed up her life in Victoria, moved to Sydney and bought a house, and got a job. All at a time when women predominately finished school, got married, started their families and stayed home. I remember being cared for each day by an old lady up the road. Then school started and my sister and I would walk the two miles or so to and from school by ourselves. I think this early independence and resilience set us both up quite well for the future.

A few years later my mother re-married and then went on to have three more children; another daughter and two sons. We all grew up knowing everything about Graham. While there were no secrets in the house, our lives were quite regimented; there was order, allocated chores and, perhaps most telling, a small replica of a ship's bell in the kitchen. When my mother wanted something done, she would ring once for Louise, twice for me and three times for my younger sister Michelle. (And I would love to argue here that perhaps the exclusion of my brothers was based on their sex but, in reality, they were just toddlers at the time.)

Maybe because of my childhood experiences, and the stories of my mother and father ·I grew up listening to, I always felt drawn to and destined for a career in the armed forces. And it must have been something about the ship's bell that led me, in particular, to the Navy in 1979 when I was in Year 11. Or perhaps it was the World War II movie *Ship Ahoy* (complete with Nazis, ocean liners, the main character tap-dancing messages in Morse code to a United States (US) agent, and an uncredited appearance from Frank Sinatra), or maybe just an aversion to the polyester mint-green uniform that Army women wore in the 1970s and early 1980s. But I do recall thinking the Navy uniform for women was the most military-looking of all the Services! That said, it was arguably more like the local women's seniors bowling club attire!

Whatever the reason, I went along to a recruiting centre in Parramatta, Sydney, and sweetly asked the sailor behind the desk what jobs could I do in the Navy after I completed Year 12. He said I could be a driver, a steward, a cook or a writer, which were some of the few categories then allocated to female sailors. *OK*, I thought, *sounds interesting!*

Well, nothing really stood out as being awesome, but my interest in the Navy remained and so, the next year, in 1980, I wrote to the recruiting centre, gave them my Year 12 mid-year exams results and they sent me an application for Supplementary List (short service commission officer entry). This form of entry, which only allowed women and some men to join for a period of nine years, was the only avenue at that time for women joining as officers, and usually offered as a result of completing Year 12 and passing four subjects, including maths and English. Men were generally appointed on the General List, a life-time commission. Occupations on offer were logistics, communications or administration. That sounded a little more promising than what the sailor at the recruiting centre had outlined, but I had no idea what an officer was, or did. I merely completed the application and made my way through the various testing phases to an officer selection panel.

I really had no clue as to what I was committing myself. I rocked up looking (I thought) glamourous in a white suit Mum had made for my Year 12 graduation, long, blonde hair out over my shoulders. (A few years later, one of our Admirals, who had been the chair of my selection panel, told me he only let me into the Navy because of my hair!) Quite frankly, I didn't even know a bow from a stern! The senior female officer on the panel told me outright she thought I was only joining the Navy to find a husband. I was bemused but promptly responded that it was the last thing on my mind (which it was). What I actually said was something like, 'I don't think I need to join the

Navy to find a husband.' On reflection, that probably sounded a bit pompous, but I actually meant that was the furthest thing from my mind. Hello, it was 1980—I wanted a career!

I'll expand on the story that unfolded after getting through that first selection panel in the following chapters. What I will say here is that, back in 1980, I had no idea of the many obstacles, challenges and opportunities I would face to make me the person I am today. I didn't know then that my career would take some significant turns and enable me to find my passion and my purpose so early in the journey.

What I learnt quickly was that I would be navigating unchartered waters for female officers, sometimes sailing against the wind, but always forging ahead in claiming my rights to equality, my rights to enjoy a career unfettered by exclusions due to gender and, ultimately, shaping, influencing and leading change and transformation on women's full participation and representation in global peace and security efforts.

Over time, through my experiences and challenges, I developed a voice for women affected by violence in the military. I built a credible reputation as an expert in gender perspectives and the role of women in the military. I authored many articles, and even a chapter for the inaugural *Oxford Handbook on Women, Peace and Security* in 2018. I became an in-demand keynote speaker, and began mentoring and coaching other women in male-dominated sectors. I've been recognised with various national awards for women, I am an ambassador for various organisations representing women's interests, and I also serve as a non-executive director for the International Women's Development Agency, focused on women's equality and development.

I became that woman I couldn't see way back in 1981.

MY VISION AND MISSION

I am very proud of my Naval service, although I often felt like a square peg in a round hole. As you'll read through this book, my experiences in the Navy created some confusing emotions: sadness, anger and disappointment for the first half and some later aspects of my career, but also joy, happiness and excitement for the opportunities, roles and positions that enabled me, over some thirty-eight years, to contribute to the more positive changes for women in our armed forces, our society and our communities. I feel very privileged to contribute to the defence of Australia, its national interests, including those in overseas conflicts. While I did not know or appreciate the risks I would become exposed to in the early years, I am not bitter and nor do I regret any decisions, actions or sacrifices I made for myself, my family and my service.

As a thought leader, advocate for women's rights and equality, and practitioner in woman's meaningful participation, my belief is that women are not free when any woman is unfree. My vision is a world where women are respected and valued, have full equality, and are empowered to live their lives freely and unfettered. My mission is to inspire, lead and empower women to live self-determined lives, reach their full potential, realise their dreams, and become free to make their own choices in all aspects of their lives. I credit my naval service to leading me to my purpose in life.

I hope that in writing this book and sharing my story, women of all ages and stages who are working hard and tirelessly in male-dominated industries with similar challenges to those I have faced will gain hope and faith that a time will come when they are no longer judged against the standards of men, where no gender pay gap exists, where gender advisers are no longer required, and where gender perspective becomes a common consideration in the development and implementation of all policy and practice that affects both women and men.

I decided to call the book *Against the Wind*, as a reflection of my view that in aspiring to 'be what you can't see', and to successfully navigate your way around a male-dominated workplace, you have to take charge of yourself and your career—and sometimes that means separating yourself from the pack and choosing a different tack.

What you may see, before you read this book, is the way you have become conditioned to your environment, one which may have certain boundaries that may not allow you to be yourself and fulfil your potential. My hope is you see a different way after reading this book.

Jennifer Wittwer, CSM
Canberra, Australia, 2020

Introduction

Smooth waters never made a skilled sailor.

Franklin D. Roosevelt

As I mention in the preface, this book is a mixture of my story and the practical advice I've developed from this experience for all women as they navigate their journey in male-dominated professions.

At first I thought I would just write my memoir: the story of one woman's career in the very male-dominated RAN. After all, my life has been one of many experiences and being the 'first' in many instances. I have had my share of hard lessons, hard knocks, amazing opportunities and achievements — way beyond my expectations.

Then I realised I had so much to share with women today — women like you, who work in male-dominated professions. I can share experiences and learnings that have as much relevance for you now as they did for me. Why? Because I see the same challenges now that existed for me throughout my lengthy career!

So, I thought, why not share what I learnt about not just surviving, but actually maximising opportunities and thriving in my chosen field. This led me to the purpose of this book: to give you some practical strategies and tips on how to feel more empowered in your profession, to feel more energised, to lead more purposefully and to do it all with passion.

When I joined the Women's Royal Australian Naval Service (WRANS) in 1981, as what is known now as a maritime logistics officer, I was by all accounts a young, naive and impressionable woman. I honestly had no idea what I was doing. As I mentioned in the preface, I didn't know a bow from a stern. (Well, that actually didn't matter back then because women weren't allowed to serve on ships!)

I joined in a class of about forty young women and men (of which only eight were women) on short service commissions. Only two classes per year were recruited. We completed our training at RANC, in Jervis Bay Territory south of Sydney. This was also the training centre for young male officers on permanent commissions completing diplomas of applied science (this was the main method of entry for male officers prior to the Australian Defence Force Academy (ADFA) opening in 1986). So already we women were in the minority. At that time, women comprised only about 7 per cent of the total Navy workforce.

'Be brave,' I said to myself. *Set some important goals*, I thought. *Surely this will tide me through*—and, ultimately, it did. At the time, the only senior female logistics officers I remember—Denise Smith, Jenny Lloyd, and Lila Bilsborough—left the service sometime in the mid-1980s to early 1990s. There were no other women working in logistics senior enough to me to look up to and aspire to be like, particularly later in the 1990s when I was qualifying as a charge logistics officer (meaning I could go on to serve as the head of the logistics department and go to sea).

That said, some amazing women were in communications and administration who had achieved the rank of Commander or Captain (then the ceiling rank for women) before they retired: Barbara McLeod, June Baker (the commander from my selection panel who suggested I was looking for a husband), Sandy Coulson, Sue Manning, Sue Jones, Liz Cole and Ros Keysell. Another notable female leader was Carolyn Brand, a mine warfare officer recruited from the RN (the United Kingdom's (UK) Navy) in the 1980s in an employment category that didn't yet exist for women in our Navy. And I appreciated them paving the way for the next generation.

However, I was in logistics, and women had only been offered this occupation from about 1979. I had to have the vision to fuel the necessary determination to succeed. I needed tenacity and just plain grit in spades to make a career in the Navy, and I wanted to thrive, not just survive!

I had to see past the systemic barriers, the discrimination and the inequalities that existed at the time to see myself in the future, having reached my full potential, having made my mark. And this was what I set out to do!

Thankfully, the introduction of the Sex Discrimination Act in 1984 was the beginning of change. Women like me were able to ride the groundswell of that change over the following thirty years or so and become the role models for the women who followed us.

Throughout the following thirty-five years, women have had to step up and be those 'firsts' as the historical chains of systemic inequality slowly dropped away.

BE WHAT YOU CAN'T SEE

I touch on my mantra that women need to be what they can't see in the preface, but let me expand on the idea here. One of the most common expressions we hear as women in male-dominated professions is that 'you can't be what you can't see', because women, of course, need role models. Only then we can see what we can achieve. Right?

Even some high-profile Australian women, themselves the 'first' in their careers, perpetuate the myth that 'if you can't see it, you can't be it'. This sentiment has long been behind the push to encourage more women into occupations and roles previously denied them due to gender restrictions. I completely understand why this exists; however, at some stage, some women actually have to be the 'first'. In the absence of role models, you need to be what you can't see.

Let me share an example. In 1996, I hit a major milestone. I served on a Navy ship as the senior logistics officer (by the way, one of only two women in a crew of 212, but more on that later!) and successfully completed a full tour of duty. I was one of the first two female logistic officers to do so. And 1996 wasn't that long ago!

I had become the role model for the more junior women behind me. Being in this role also meant I had to excel, shine and stand out, because of the high expectations on me to perform—at the same standard as the men! (I'll talk about this myth later in the book!)

But, for me, I couldn't wait to see it, to be it. I had to be what I couldn't see.

That was then.

And this is now.

Even today, however, women still face many challenges around their participation and representation—sexual harassment, systemic barriers to promotion, and toxic cultures of masculinity, to name a few. And a plethora of conferences, seminars and workshops are aimed at giving you the skills and inspiration to forge careers in male-dominated professions. From what I have seen, women's attendance levels at these events clearly indicates a need and desire to learn more about how they can confront these challenges and rise above them.

I know many women and men in our professions are resistant to the very notion of any special measures that assist women to gain traction in these areas. Usually this resistance is based on myths and misconceptions about quotas, targets, equality versus equity, gender perspective, merit, and even the need for diversity.

Many argue that women's participation is irrelevant to the organisation's outcomes—the successful applicant is always the best person for the job. However, we know many of these organisations still have systems and processes skewed heavily towards a historically masculine construct that can exclude women.

The result of this is that we remain underrepresented at senior levels, we don't have the role models, or enough role models, to aspire to and be inspired by, and we struggle to compete with our male colleagues. Perhaps you've considered leaving your profession because the 'boys' club' has become too much. You see the senior leadership team consisting mostly of men. You think you can't be what you can't see.

Is this because you lack the qualifications or criteria for the job or promotion? I don't think so. What I do believe is that you may not have a really defined sense of purpose. You may need to grab the opportunities to develop vision, direction and self-awareness, to then step up and be the 'first'.

I would ask you this: is the 'to be it, you have to see it' approach just a limiting belief we impose on ourselves to excuse our inability as individual women to challenge the status quo in those organisations?

What I suggest in this book is that, in fact, women who join male-dominated professions do indeed hold the key to their own future.

You can learn to not only survive the hegemonic masculinity in your workplace but, indeed, step up and thrive with clear aspirations, a strong sense of self, and energy and passion to make a difference.

You just need to use the right keys to unlock the power within. You can empower yourself to be the person you need to be, to do what you need to do, and to have the results or outcomes you're looking for.

I provide the keys to being what you can't see through the chapters in part II of this book, but let me say this for now: the place to start is recognising that you need to say yes and tackle the 'firsts' that continue to arise for women. Many of you will have to accept that you will become the role models for future generations. It's a tough gig but someone has to do it. These 'firsts' should be acknowledged and celebrated. You can be what you can't see if you are prepared to be in the spotlight, to make the necessary noise, to cheer on and support your tribe to do the same.

MY FOCUS THROUGH THIS BOOK

This book is designed to help you to:

- overcome your feelings of being disempowered in a masculine culture

- confront your self-talk (such as those associated with imposter syndrome) that may be holding you back

- stop being afraid of becoming the 'first' in something, and hiding behind the idea of equality as a reason not to acknowledge that 'first'

- overcome your fear of expressing your femininity and celebrate being a woman leader.

I'm not asking you to take on a Herculean task. I'm merely suggesting that some inner reflection to gain external change will create the new direction you need to take to succeed in your career. You may see this as a personal development journey and, in some ways, it is. But invariably it will lead you to greater clarity around your ability to not only survive but really thrive in a profession and workplace that you are deservedly serving in.

A word of warning: Often, the greatest barrier for women is to stand up, step up, make noise, make change, and be the 'first'. Not only can men resent that women are doing it 'just because they are women', but also women must overcome the self-beliefs and limitations they impose on themselves.

I know some of you may experience the 'tall poppy syndrome'—I know I spent many years internally fighting the patriarchy for my space and right to be where I was—and you worry about what your peers, and others, may think of you. You often also succumb to 'imposter syndrome', because, you wonder, what makes you so special? What makes you stand out?

But, honestly, if you want to stay in your chosen profession, if you want to thrive and not just survive, then you have to get over these negative feelings and thoughts.

Like me, you have to learn to own your space. You have to constantly use self-talk that focuses on your value and worth. You have to say to yourself, 'I've got this!'

I know and have experienced many of the challenges that women face in masculine environments. I served in the RAN for thirty-eight years, constantly proving that I was worthy of being there.

I spent my entire career supporting women to achieve their full potential. I was at times a square peg in a round hole, but I never wavered from my purpose: to serve and empower women. This wasn't easy—in fact, it was damn hard—but I persevered, every day, every week, every year.

Something happened to me early on in my career (and I talk about this in more detail later in the book) that defined who I was, that gave me the clarity I needed to succeed in the face of adversity, obstacles and, quite frankly, resistance by men against my presence, just because I was a woman.

I made the decision to not be a victim, but to use this and many other experiences to learn and grow, and to ultimately be what I couldn't see.

I learnt to find the silver linings and build resilience. I took advantage of opportunities that were presented to me and I created new pathways. Along the way, I learnt so much about what you need to do to survive, thrive and prosper in your careers. And this is what I want to share with you.

I will take you on a journey as I show you that you *can* be what you can't see. Along the way, I will share with you my personal experiences and stories that made me who I am today. I will be brutally honest so that this might provide you with a benchmark or standard against which you can assess your own challenges and obstacles in your profession. I hope that you will see yourself in me, as I also see myself in so many women. I hope this book makes you reflect on what you are already doing well and what is the missing piece, or pieces, that could make all the difference.

Working in male-dominated professions creates a difficult pathway for many women. Perhaps you sometimes feel you can navigate it easily; other times, perhaps you need support. Only you can create the change you want to see and be. Only you can calm yourself and arm yourself with the necessary tools to enable you to be what you can't see.

I did it.

Now it's time for you to take control of your own destiny and make it work for you.

HOW THIS BOOK IS ORGANISED

As you make your way through this book, I firstly ask you to reflect on the quotes at the start of each chapter. These have been specifically chosen to reflect the purpose and intent of the chapter and to provide motivation and inspiration. These can easily become affirmations for your new directions and aspirations.

In the chapters in the first part of this book, I provide some 'herstory' around the current course, and the challenges for women that exist in male-dominated professions. If you like, however, you can go directly to the chapters in part II to learn about my strategies on how to overcome the challenges and obstacles and find new opportunities. This is the critical part of the book, organised around the five strategies from my Be What You Can't See model (shown in the following figure).

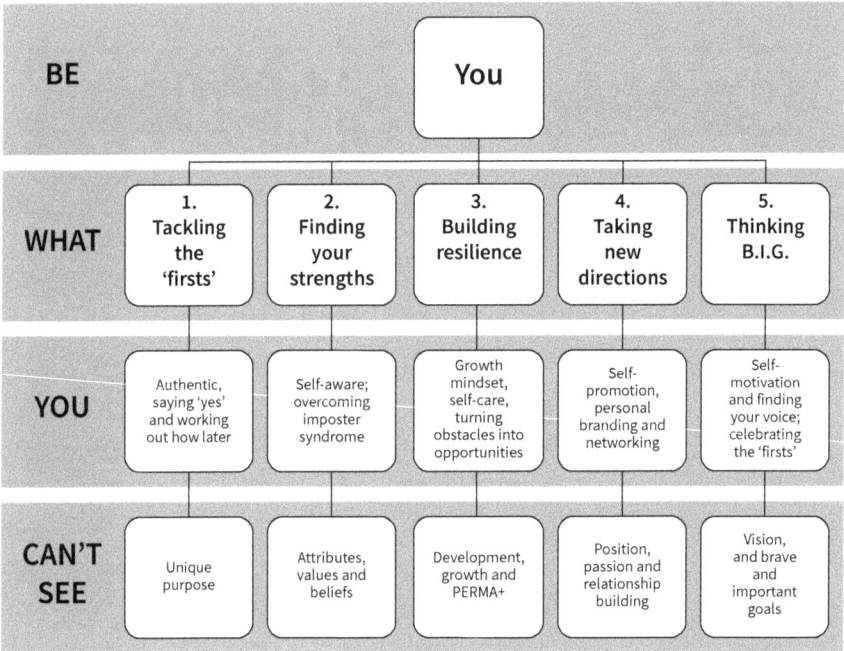

BE			You			
WHAT		1. Tackling the 'firsts'	2. Finding your strengths	3. Building resilience	4. Taking new directions	5. Thinking B.I.G.
YOU		Authentic, saying 'yes' and working out how later	Self-aware; overcoming imposter syndrome	Growth mindset, self-care, turning obstacles into opportunities	Self-promotion, personal branding and networking	Self-motivation and finding your voice; celebrating the 'firsts'
CAN'T SEE		Unique purpose	Attributes, values and beliefs	Development, growth and PERMA+	Position, passion and relationship building	Vision, and brave and important goals

As you can see in the figure, my five strategies are:

- Tackling the 'firsts'
- Finding your strengths
- Building resilience
- Taking new directions
- Thinking B.I.G.

See chapters 7 to 12 for more on each of these strategies.

Finally, in the chapters in part III, I outline the ways in which you can take what you have learnt and use it in your profession. This will help you make your mark, whatever that looks like.

I have included key points at the end of each chapter, so you're clear on the main message for reference later. My hope is that this book becomes dog-eared, written on and in, and 'used' as you move through the strategies. What is contained in this book will help you overcome any fears you might have that your chosen career is not the right one for you, and help you understand that, in fact, you can make yourself the right one for it.

Finally, and I really want to shout this from the top of the closest building, stop hiding behind the veil of 'equality'. By this I mean, stop wanting to blend into the masculine landscape because you think that's the only way to succeed. Own the fact you are a woman. Act with authenticity, and this will be your key to serving with purpose.

Stop being afraid to celebrate your achievements. Until women are participating at higher levels in your workforce, be proud of the difference that you make as a woman.

Use this book to stop being afraid of being you.

If I can help you do any or some of these things, then I will have achieved my purpose.

MY TOP 5 TIPS

1. In the absence of role models, 'be what you can't see'.

2. Grab the opportunities to develop vision, direction and self-awareness, to then step up and be the 'first'.

3. You can empower yourself to be the person you need to be, to do what you need to do, and to create the results or outcomes you're looking for.

4. Use self-talk about your value and worth and say to yourself, 'I've got this!'

5. Own the fact you are a woman. Act with authenticity, and this will be your key to serving with purpose.

Part One

THE CURRENT COURSE

We must free ourselves of the hope that the sea will ever rest.
We must learn to sail in high winds.

Aristotle Onassis, Shipping Magnate

One
It's a man's world

I don't mind being in a man's world,
as long as I can be a woman in it.

Marilyn Monroe

In 2013, aged fifty-one, I deployed to Afghanistan as a military gender adviser to the NATO Resolute Support Mission. I know, you're probably thinking, *Wow, who would do that?* Right?

Well, I did it for two reasons. One, it was an amazing opportunity to work on gender perspective in operations. (As I explain further in chapter 4, while this sounds technical, it's actually pretty simple once you start asking the right questions and looking at things with the right perspective.) Two, I would gain some credibility as a female military veteran through being awarded the associated medals.

This latter point was important to me because, before the 1990s, Australia was in a period of peace with only a few military men deploying to UN missions. This meant the only personnel wearing medals really were our older, mostly male, Vietnam War-era veterans. Of course, I acknowledge the many (female) nurses who served in the wars of the 20th century and also earned their medals. Most of my contemporaries, however, women and men, didn't have any medals except for the one that recognised long service.

Then the 1990s and 2000s saw the Australian military involved in a number of conflicts and UN humanitarian and peacekeeping operations. These included Timor-Leste, Solomon Islands, Iraq, the Gulf War, Rwanda and, of course, Afghanistan.

All of a sudden, lots of young people were wearing medals. And, all of a sudden, my contemporaries with medals were viewed differently. They had 'been to war' like our forebears. They were doing exactly what we had all been trained to do. Fight.

These changes initially did not necessarily include women. Some Navy women snuck through because, around the same time, the government had lifted the gender restrictions on combat-related roles. Women were starting to serve on ships, and on many of the ships deployed to those conflicts. And these women were earning medals. So, in 2013, joining the ranks of those wearing medals was important to me.

Later, women deploying became more normal and I think it would be safe to say there aren't many women now in the military without a few, if not a lot, of medals. But you know what? Even as late as 2016, many people in the Australian community, most of them men, would question women about their medals—for example, the medals they were wearing on Anzac Day. They would approach women who were excitedly preparing to march, and ask something like, 'Why are you wearing your [father's/brother's/husband's] medals on your left?' (Meaning, over the left breast.) 'You should be wearing relatives' medals on the right.' I have witnessed accusations such as this and the ignorance of these men was mind-blowing to me and all the women who experienced this treatment.

These sorts of comments just brought home to us the fact that many still see the military as a 'boy zone'—one where, like social expectations and gender stereotypes dictated in the past, men go to war, and the women stay home and keep the 'home fires burning.'

Seriously, I was very disappointed. Women have been serving in the Australian military, with distinction, courage and tenacity, in various capacities, since at least World War One. The brave military nurses killed by the Japanese armed forces on Bangka Island in 1942 are just one example of many. Numerous books have been written about or by women in the military, or at least the famous ones (such as Nancy Wake, *The White Mouse*). Over the last two decades, recruiting campaigns for the military have promoted women's participation. Women have marched in Anzac Day parades and others. Women are seen out and about in uniform.

What the hell?! This is 2019!

Now, because of my service in Afghanistan and in other roles, I had accrued seven medals, more than my then partner John, an Army Armored Corp officer, who had been deployed to Lebanon in the early 1980s with the UN peacekeeping mission and had completed over twenty-five years' service. He has four medals. Indeed, my father, Graham, a RAAF pilot in the 1950s and 1960s, was awarded three medals, for service in Malaysia, National Service and the Australian Defence Medal (ADM) for military service. And I shouldn't let an opportunity pass to also highlight that my mother received a retrospective ADM for her service in the RAAF in the 1950s!

I was ahead of the game! But many other women were playing also.

In 2017, Kellie Dadds, an amazing Army veteran, and the Women Veterans Network Australia created the 'By the Left' campaign to raise public awareness about women veterans, their service and their medals.[1] The campaign had well and truly gained traction in time for the Anzac Day march in 2018. At marches around Australia, the Returned Services League (the organisers of these marches) promoted women's participation by creating a formation just for woman at the head of each parade.

This was huge, the publicity was extensive, and the response by women to march was overwhelming, with some coming out of self-imposed purgatory to support their sisters-in-arms.

Then we had the naysayers — mostly men — saying things like, 'Why do women need their own formation? They should march with their own units if they want gender equality', and so on. You can imagine. Yet the irony of men having their own formations for decades was completely lost on them.

I just wondered why they felt threatened.

I also saw that, for so many, equality meant being the same — or, rather, equality meant women being the same as men.

---

1 See https://www.dva.gov.au/about-dva/publications/vetaffairs/vol-33-no4-summer-2017/their-medals-are-rightly-left/ for more information.

But back to the assumptions about women's medals and their participation in the armed forces: why is it still so strange to many that women serve in the military, or police, or other uniformed services?

Well, it comes down to these professions being classified 'male-dominated', and the consequences of this affect women significantly.

WHAT IS A MALE-DOMINATED PROFESSION?

And why is this even still a reality in 2019?

I recently read a 2018 report by Catalyst (a global non-profit working with some of the world's most powerful chief executive officers and leading companies to build workplaces that work for women). They suggested that male-dominated occupations are those that comprise 25 per cent or fewer women — that is, one in four workers in these occupations are women.

I suppose that's a fair call, because anything higher might actually get closer to a gender balance.

This kind of low representation is definitely seen in the Australian military, where women's participation in 2019 is sitting at around 18.6 per cent. And it's not just Australia where this is the case. In 2017, women made up 16 per cent of active-duty personnel in the US armed forces. Across NATO member nations, women's participation ranges from 0.6 per cent (Turkey) to 20 per cent (Hungary), according to NATO statistics from 2016[2].

The Australian Bureau of Statistics (ABS) 2016 census showed that some jobs seem to remain consistently 'male' and 'female'. The top six traditionally male occupations — carpenters and joiners (99.3 per cent male), motor mechanics (98.6 per cent), electricians (98.5 per cent), truck drivers (96.7 per cent), construction managers (96.7 per cent) and storepersons (92.5 per cent) — remain heavily skewed towards men. (Note that a storeperson handles products being received or dispatched by stores, and are responsible for handling and packing goods. They are different from a sales assistant, a role that the

---

2   NATO. 2016. 'Summary of the National Reports of NATO Member and Partner Nations to the NATO Committee on Gender Perspectives'.

ABS 2016 census figures showed is skewed more towards women, with 67.6 per cent female workers.)

For women, the top six occupations were child carers (95.1 per cent female), receptionists (94.8 per cent), education aides (90.4 per cent), registered nurses (89.2 per cent) and office managers (88.2 per cent). To see more information about the breakdown of occupations by gender based on the 2016 census, go to www.abs.gov.au.

But let's move on from statistics alone. According to the Collins Dictionary, a male-dominated organisation is one in which men have most of the power and influence. So, I argue that greater than 25 per cent participation from women alone cannot possibly be the tipping point!

This seems to be the aspect of male-dominated professions most overlooked by women who want to mainstream with men, and by those who believe equality means being the same as men.

The problem is, no matter the breakdown of women and men employees, these organisations can be fraught with masculine and gendered stereotypes, a lack of female role models (particularly in niche and emerging occupations), a difficulty in balancing work–life relationships, and the perception that women are less ambitious than their male counterparts. Accordingly, women in these professions are more likely to abandon their careers mid-stream — and so reinforcing that these problems and stereotypes make it difficult for women to excel.

Studies show that women also face higher levels of sexual harassment, and they also have fewer mentoring opportunities. I don't know about you, but I suffered from both, as did many of my female peers. It strikes me as odd (to say the least) that, firstly, these things continue even in 2019 and, secondly, organisations are not necessarily taking any action to address them.

Of course, it was great to see (former Australian Sex Discrimination Commissioner) Elizabeth Broderick's report, released in June 2019, on the internal culture of the New South Wales Police Force.[3]

---

3   Broderick, Elizabeth. 2019. 'Review into the NSW Police Promotions System, 2019'. See http://elizabethbroderick.com.au/wp-content/uploads/Final-Report-into-the-NSW-Police-Promotions-System.pdf.

(In 2018, women constituted 27.6 per cent of the police workforce.) Her report concluded that:

- Women were forced to conform to a masculine culture to find a position in the organisation.

- They had to modify their behaviours and were constantly trying to 'prove themselves' in order to be 'accepted' and 'taken seriously'.

- Female officers felt cliques, in-crowds and the 'boys' club' formed a barrier to promotion.

- A high level of sexual harassment existed in the workplace.

- Women who were taking advantage of flexible work practices faced discrimination in the promotions system.

These findings led to the NSW Police Commissioner vowing to bring an end to the 'boys' club' and 'male-dominated bygone era', to bring in a more equitable promotions system that removed discrimination against officers working part-time and flexibly, and to address sexual harassment.

This was the best news ever for women in the NSW Police Force. But given that Ms Broderick also conducted a similar review in the treatment of women in the Australian military in 2012[4], with similar outcomes and recommendations, it seems that contemporary male-dominated workplaces everywhere need an overhaul. They need to be Brodericked!

Similarly, a 2019 report by Rapid Context[5], a Canberra-based consultancy, which examined the defence industry workforce, identified a number of 'push' factors for women leaving roles in this industry. These included:

- experiencing sexism, sexual harassment or gender bias

---

4   Australian Human Rights Commission. 2012. 'Review into the Treatment of Women in the Australian Defence Force; Phase 2 Report.' See https://defence.humanrights.gov.au/sites/default/files/adf-complete.pdf.

5   Rapid Context. 2019. 'Growing the defence industry workforce: Attracting and retaining women with critical skills and trades'. July 2019.

- isolation and a lack of mentoring opportunities

- feeling discriminated against on the basis of gender

- finding it difficult to adapt to a 'male-dominated 'culture

- facing perpetual barriers such as feeling underestimated, subject to implicit bias or unbalanced power dynamics.

Perhaps I digress. But the last point brings me back to men's power and influence.

This can operate in male-dominated professions, organisations, workplaces and even countries. A good example is the Ukraine, a beautiful country which is at the time of writing experiencing conflict in the Crimea, with a heavily patriarchal society, social structure, governance and reform.

A lot of work has been done in the past three to four years to address gender discrimination in the Ukraine's defence and security sector. And yet, as late as mid-2019, the newly elected President, Volodymyr Zelensky, described beautiful women as part of the country's 'brand'. His comments prompted the hashtags #Iamnotyourbrand and #Iamnotyourtourismbrand, with leading rights activists calling the comments sexist.

So, ladies, for those of you who still think that all in your profession treat you equally and without discrimination, the evidence seems to demonstrate otherwise.

I wonder if you have ever really thought about how you operate in your workplace? In order to fit in, did you become 'beige', 'one of the boys'?

This worries me because if women are doing this, they are potentially buying into the masculine culture that perpetuates historical masculine benchmarks and standards (and I'll talk about these a little later in this chapter). Like I've said previously, these 'standards' mean women have to fit into the male construct.

But it's time to fight back. It's time for women to take their rightful place, to demand equality on the basis of new benchmarks, standards and norms.

CULTURE CLUB

As the NSW Police Force case study shows, a masculine culture prevails in male-dominated workplaces that causes women disproportionate discrimination and more difficulty in seeking promotion and advancement. It's quite possible that this kind of culture is more prevalent at times when an organisation is changing—when occupations that previously excluded women, for example, are opening up to them, and when the rules change.

I had an interesting experience when I served on HMAS *Swan*, a Vietnam War–era destroyer escort, in 1996. As I mention in the introduction, I was the senior maritime logistics officer, one of two women in a crew of 212, and a part of the ship's executive leadership team. It was early days in having women serve on ships, and these days were not without some significant issues because, in many ways, the culture of the organisation and its people had not been brought along with this change.

The culture on board the ship was mostly fine, brought about by good leadership by the Commanding Officer. Generally, the ship's company treated my female colleague and me with courtesy and respect. My team gave me the utmost professional and personal support, and I believed that I fitted well into that environment.

One of my peers, a fellow officer of the same rank, didn't seem to think the same, however. He would constantly undermine my decisions and authority (oh, and, by the way, he wasn't a logistics officer), try to tell me what to do—despite being the same rank—and bully me into doing so. He called me names in front of junior staff, like 'blond bimbo' or SWOD ('sailor without a dick').

My only consolation was that those who heard him say these things thought he was a right twat anyway (actually, their words about him were harsher than mine).

I reported his behaviour to the commander, implying I would report higher up the chain of command if he wasn't dealt with. I just wanted his behaviour to stop. Well, to cut a long story short, he did apologise to me—but also said that's how he spoke to all women! After I picked my jaw up off the deck, I said, 'This is 1996! You can't talk to women like that.' I was flabbergasted.

Along with this, some other incidents unrelated to me but to do with his behaviour also indicated he had lost the respect of the ship's company. But … a few weeks later, I was collating the annual performance reports for the executive leadership team (one of the perks of being the logistics officer). To my dismay, I discovered that both he and I had been assessed by the commander similarly, with us both meeting assessment criteria and achieving a high score, and with no mention of his actions and subsequent counselling as demonstrating, perhaps, a level of leadership below that expected of his rank and position.

And, of course, my performance had been exemplary! In truth, it had, and I was very disappointed—and even more so when the following year he was promoted, and I was not. And then to top it off, the second assessor, the commander's commander, wrote that I was the worst performing logistics officer in the fleet. This was despite me meeting all operational objectives, keeping the ship afloat, the ship's company paid and fed (food is the single most important element of ship life), and developing the implementation plan for the ship's decommissioning that followed soon after.

I suspect it was because this second assessor was totally unimpressed that, in my downtime, I would sit in the mess and knit, and he witnessed this once after we had completed an exhausting operational workup. He must have forgotten that sailors used to knit in the old, old days.

Anyway, I'm not meaning to big note myself or my performance at that time, but it certainly didn't warrant that assessment. To me, this was just indicative of the boys' club culture that prevailed at that time, when men (and their wives) didn't want women at sea, all while women were now joining them in occupations to which they had previously been denied.

I wondered, what was their problem and why did they feel threatened?

TOXIC MASCULINITY

I know the RAN is built upon a long and proud history emerging from the RN, and it has a strong traditional base of service and professionalism. This cannot be denied. It has always had the highest standards of training and expectations of its people. It has created well-respected and inspirational leaders and has always been known as the 'senior service'.

The majority of the men in the Navy are a credit to it, the country and themselves. I have no doubts about that.

I was proud to join the WRANS in 1981 and then, in 1984, transition into the RAN, colloquially known as the 'men's service'. I think for men, this initial transition didn't matter much because women remained employed in restricted categories, they didn't serve at sea and didn't deploy — they just got on providing support as they had done historically.

But as I describe earlier in this chapter, the later lifting of gender restrictions on combat-related roles (in the early 1990s) and combat roles (in 2011) suddenly meant women were being recruited into, and trained in, the men's employment specialisations and were being posted to sea to meet service obligations.

All of a sudden, men were confronted with women engineers, technicians, ship drivers and pilots, who were also then 'taking' positions at sea.

And their wives were also confronted! Lordy lord, they would write to the Fleet Commander to tell him it wasn't appropriate to have women on their husband's ships — because he might have an affair or sexual relations! Because all women I know who went to sea went for those reasons!

Seriously? This reminded me of my selection board when joining the Navy, when I was accused of only joining to find a husband!

Eeeek! No, I'm eighteen and want to see the world.

Okay, so it was a man's world. This remained the case through the 1990s and 2000s as Navy men had to adapt to having women on their teams.

But what of other male-dominated professions, and the long and tightly held masculinity so prevalent in them? Is this masculinity toxic? Or is it normal? Or is 'normal' actually toxic?

Well, if studies show that male-dominated professions have higher rates of sexual harassment and violence, then potentially those professions, as witnessed by the outcomes of the NSW Police review, are actually exhibiting toxic masculinity.

To quote a reliable source—Wikipedia—the concept of toxic masculinity is referring to certain norms of masculine behaviour that are associated with harm to society and to men themselves:

> Traditional stereotypes of men as socially dominant, along with related traits such as misogyny and homophobia, can be considered 'toxic' due in part to their promotion of violence, including sexual assault and domestic violence. The socialization of boys often normalizes violence, such as in the saying 'boys will be boys' with regard to bullying and aggression.

(In fairness to Wikipedia, other more notable dictionaries cite similar phraseology.)

Of course, these traits were not always called 'toxic masculinity'. In the book *Angry White Men*, US academic Michael Kimmel describes the anger of men whose unrealistic expectations of power and dominance are not met. The book was first published in 2013, but the term 'toxic masculinity' did not become widely used until late 2017, after accusations of sexual harassment and assault against Hollywood producer Harvey Weinstein were made public. (Remember #MeToo? I'll talk about that in chapter 5.)

So, what does this mean for women in male-dominated organisations? Have we blindly accepted (toxic) masculinity as an inherent part of the job, and not sought to fight the patriarchy because we just wanted to keep that job?

Now we know this masculinity is about men's control of power and influence, and, when threatened, it can become 'toxic'. I wonder now how you, as part of the 25 per cent (or lower) representation in male-dominated professions, feel about a seemingly blind acceptance of this culture. I wonder if we do so in order to protect our right to a career, our right to advance (on merit, of course), and our right to be seen as, and be, equal with men (more on equality in chapter 4).

Something to ask yourself.

MASCULINE STEREOTYPES

You've probably read (or at least heard about) *Men are from Mars, Women are from Venus* by John Grey, so you get the whole bit about psychological differences between men and women. But we also know that, historically, we have been brought up with specific *social* gender stereotypes that have previously constrained women to certain roles in our homes, communities and work.

I mean, I joined the Navy only two years after the government removed the requirement for pregnant women to leave the service. We have evolved so much and so well since then. But during my career, when employment and parts of the culture were changing as more and more women joined, the stereotypes persisted.

I experienced this in 1986, when I was on the staff as a Sub-Lieutenant at the RANC at Jervis Bay, south of Sydney. Set in the most beautiful, pristine national park, with white sandy beaches and blue waters (just trying to distract you!), at that time, as well as training short service commissioned officers, the College was an academic campus for male students undertaking Diplomas of Applied Science (this was before ADFA in Canberra, which opened that year).

Every year, the cadets would do some sort of adventure training—sailing, gliding, or trekking (on the Kokoda Trail, in Papua New Guinea (PNG)). They were looking for staff to accompany them and I volunteered for the Kokoda Trek. I was young, fit and able. I was an emerging leader. I was capable of looking after myself and others, so what could go wrong?

Well, you'd think I'd asked to nominate for prime minister.

The problem was I would be the first military woman to do this trek.

The officer-in-charge, Lieutenant Graeme Pedley, RAN, was more than happy for me to go as long as I met the physical standards. But some of the young male officer trainees (midshipmen, or the most junior-ranked officers) thought and said—to me and others—things like, 'She can't come, she won't make it, she's a woman'. Well, yes, I was, last time I looked. They also argued, 'It will be too hard to accommodate her at the army barracks over there'. Okay, in fairness, at that time the PNG Army didn't have any women.

But, really, they didn't raise anything that couldn't be overcome. So, did their concerns bear fruit? Of course not. Yes, there were some interesting and amusing moments at the barracks and along the trail. Yes, I got sick along the way as we all did, but I kept going as I reflected on what it must have been like for our soldiers in World War Two. They didn't have anyone to carry their pack when they weren't well.

That thought did not stop one of the midshipmen when he fell ill, however. We all became ill at some point. But whereas I just picked myself up, put my pack on my back and kept going, this one particular fellow allowed one of our trusted and experienced PNG Army guides to carry his pack.

And they said I couldn't do it.

On a sidenote, Graeme ended up allowing more than just me (the token woman) on the trek. He was trekking in pants and, as the days wore on, and the heat and humidity got to him, he kept cutting his pants shorter and shorter. Till one day, he went too far. Needless to say, he wore a skirt for the remainder of the trek, no doubt enjoying the cool breeze. I'm sure you can imagine that no jokes about women were allowed after that!

Okay, so you might be thinking, *Yeah, but that was 1986.* Interestingly, however, masculine stereotypes continue to prevail. A 2018 Australian study[6], involving men aged 18 to 30, referred to the concept of a 'man box' and identified the following unhealthy stereotypes that are reinforced by living within this box (quoted from mensline.org.au):

- *Self-sufficiency:* Talking with others about your issues and concerns is weak; men should figure out their personal problems without asking for help.

- *Acting tough:* A guy who doesn't fight back is weak; guys should always act strong even if they feel scared and nervous.

- *Physical attractiveness:* Successful men look good; but spending too much time on your looks is not manly.

---

6   See https://mensline.org.au/wellbeing-blog/male-stereotypes-man-box/ for more information.

- *Rigid gender roles:* Men don't do household chores; men should be the financial providers for their family.

- *Heterosexuality and homophobia:* A gay guy is not a real man; straight guys should not have gay friends.

- *Hypersexuality:* A real man has as many sexual partners as possible; a real man never says no to sex.

- *Aggression and control:* Men should use violence when necessary; a man always has the final say in a relationship.

Approximately half (49 per cent) of respondents indicated that the messages they receive about 'how to be a man' supported the negative stereotypes listed in the preceding points.

However, approximately 70 per cent of respondents did not agree with these sentiments. This is a heartening indicator of shifting attitudes among young men, and these shifts are good for both themselves personally and wider society.

But it also means that the remaining 30 per cent, potentially in the general average age group in many male-dominated professions, are still susceptible to these stereotypes.

This begs the question: how much do these men influence the culture of an organisation or, at the very least, limit the organisation's ability to change and improve over time? Do you want to work with men who think like this? Are you even conscious of these stereotypes in your organisation or profession?

MALE BENCHMARKS

Finally, what about the benchmarks or standards of the profession that were created by men for men, and to which women have to conform in order to fit in, as evidenced in the NSW Police review?

Generally, equality in our professions has come to be known as women achieving 'parity with', or becoming 'equal to', men, or being 'just like the men'. I mean, you've likely said these things without even thinking about it.

But this implies that we are meeting an assumed standard, created some time ago when life was different, which in fact may not be the right standard in a contemporary context. It also implies a male standard equates to competence.

Don't get me wrong. I'm not suggesting a 'female standard' that requires all men to wear skirts. But I do believe that a more transformative standard is one where an organisation, previously and historically only employing men, adapts to having women join, rather than expecting women to adapt to it. It would mean saying we don't expect women to be the same as men; rather we will look at how women and men are different, and what needs to change in order for both women and men to enjoy the same benefits, opportunities and resources of that organisation. (Oh, just realised, now I'm talking about gender equality and mainstreaming gender consideration to create a more efficient and effective organisation!)

In my more recent roles over the past few years, I have tackled gender issues head on to get both the organisation and the people in it to confront these assumed standards and our approach to equality.

I more often than not experienced pushback from both men and women to what they perceived as affirmative action for women. For the women pushing back, they felt these actions would disadvantage men and that this would, in some way, diminish women's achievements in a male-dominated organisation. This pushback was expressed in the form of sentiments such as, 'We are as competent as the men', 'We can do the job as well as men', and 'We are equal to men'.

In my last military posting, from late 2016 to early 2018, I was seconded to the Peace and Security section of the headquarters of UN Women[7] in New York, to work as a policy specialist on peacekeeping and sexual exploitation and abuse. In that capacity, I attended a side event at the UN during the UN Security Council's annual Open Debate on Women, Peace and Security in later 2017. This event was addressing the importance of policewomen's participation in peacekeeping (currently at around 10 per cent), and how UN member states could contribute to achieving the UN's goal of 20 per cent women's participation by 2028.

---

7   UN Women is the United Nations entity for women's equality, rights and empowerment.

The highly credible and reputable speakers at this event stressed the importance and effect of women's participation on operational outcomes, specific initiatives being undertaken by the UN to double participation rates, and the relevance of gender equality in national institutions and their underlying capacity to nominate and deploy women.

However, I could not help but call out the language used by one speaker (a male police officer) justifying women's presence and ability to do the job — in national defence and security institutions and peacekeeping. He said, 'Women are as good as the men in these roles'. Again, this takes for granted that males set the standard that women have to 'meet' and are measured against. The speaker later clarified that this was how women referred to themselves, but this came as no surprise to me.

In another example, a colleague of mine, Suzanne Smith, a producer for the Australian Broadcasting Commission produced the 2014 documentary *The Gender Mission*. This highlighted the attempts by the Norwegian armed forces to 'normalise' women's inclusion, in their mission to become known as an inclusive, cohesive and unisex defence force.

The documentary follows the Norwegian Border Guard's 'gender experiment' along the nation's remote and breathtakingly beautiful northern border with Russia. In doing so, the documentary highlights quite a telling tale about how these changes in Norway, through enabling more women to take up occupations and roles they previously had not been able to, had helped minimise the instances of sexual harassment and assault, with rates comparatively low compared to other countries.

Now, I have very high regard for my Norwegian colleagues, and have no doubt the Scandinavian countries are leading on gender equality. It's always great to see women achieving 'firsts' by breaking down barriers and taking their rightful place alongside men. (In fact, the first female Admiral appointed to NATO's Military Committee, in early 2020, was a Norwegian.) It's definitely sending the message that men don't 'own' certain occupations.

But … unfortunately, there's still always a but! Footage turned to the accommodation spaces occupied by both men and women, with little to no privacy or separation. I have no problem with this. On my ship in 1996, HMAS *Swan*, and really in many instances across my career, I used men's facilities because none were available for women. As long as some semblance of privacy was achieved, this was not a problem — no biggie, as they say.

And then it (actually, two things) happened. Wait for it … drum roll. Firstly, the documentary showed footage of locker doors and walls with posters of semi- to nude photos of women. In my mind, that didn't really suggest a culture of inclusion. Rather, it suggests a culture of, 'You're coming into my space, so you have to put up with it'.

Secondly, when talking about the living arrangements, the two women in the unit said something like, 'We don't mind sharing with the boys; we're just one of the boys.'

'We're just one of the boys.' And so my argument again is that equality is not necessarily achieved just by adding women and stirring. The culture and the language used by the organisation also needs to change to demonstrate the truest form of inclusivity.

A postscript, though: I am comforted by the words of one Norwegian colleague in particular, Colonel Ingrid Gjerde, who previously commanded all Norwegian forces in Afghanistan. She was, at the time of the documentary, the head of the Military Academy and Officer Candidate School. (The Colonel inspired me to seek, and get, the gender adviser role in Afghanistan in 2013.) In the documentary she said, 'Leadership is all about building healthy cultures, and to build healthy cultures you have to respect every single person, man and woman. And then there is a zero tolerance for harassment.'

So, Norway is undoubtedly headed in the right direction.

However, the fact is we continue to use language that normalises the male standard to justify women's progression and competence in roles in traditionally male-dominated professions. And this undermines the achievement of gender equality in its truest sense.

Because of this, I'd like to set you a challenge.

Think about why you allow yourself and other women — highly educated, smart and professional women — to compare yourselves to men.

Next time you hear another woman say something like, 'I'm as competent as the men', or 'I'm equal to men', challenge them to:

- think of a more personally reaffirming statement

- think of ways to acknowledge and celebrate their competence for any position or role

- value the differences they bring to the table

- support the valid steps being taken by their profession to increase women's participation.

And, of course, if you hear yourself making or thinking these sorts of statements, challenge yourself as well. A more personally affirming statement, for example, could be 'I am an individual. I have worked hard and completed all requirements. I am a good leader and I deserve my spot as much as anyone.' The differences women bring to the table, which in our current world state is becoming more necessary, could be aspects such as humanity and compassion, two attributes not necessarily attributed to our male warriors!

MY TOP 5 TIPS

1. It's time to fight back. It's time for women to take their rightful place, and to demand equality on the basis of new benchmarks, standards and norms.

2. Equality can often come to mean parity with or 'same as' the men. This assumes male standards equate to competence. Challenge this. Women are not 'just as good as the men'.

3. Using language such as this to justify women's progression and competence in roles in traditionally male-dominated professions undermines the achievement of gender equality in its truest sense.

4. Equality is not necessarily achieved just by adding women and stirring. Equality must also come in the culture and the language used by the organisation, and it's this that will demonstrate the truest form of inclusivity.

5. You don't need to just blindly accept masculinity as an inherent part of the job.

Two

Vaginagate:
opening or closing?

If overthrowing some five thousand years of patriarchy seems like a big order, just focus on celebrating each self-respect step along the way.

Eve Ensler, author of *The Vagina Monologues*

'Vaginagate' is a term I just learned recently. If you are well read and across global news, you may have previously heard of the term, which emanated in Michigan, United States, in 2012. There, politician Lisa Brown was banned from addressing the Michigan State House for a day after she used the word 'vagina' in a debate about anti-abortion legislation.

In the debate, Brown concluded her speech as follows: 'Mr Speaker, I'm flattered that you're all so interested in my vagina, but "no" means 'no".' When the outrage and subsequent ban ensued, she responded with, 'If I can't say the word vagina, why are we legislating vaginas?'

A good point given that 'vagina' is an appropriate medical term for that part of a woman's body.

And so, the phenomenon of vaginagate was born.

Vaginagate was further amplified by the release, also in 2012, of *A Year of Biblical Womanhood* by Rachel Held Evans, which examines what it would mean to live life as a woman according to the biblical laws for a year.

Evans speaks plainly about many things addressed in the Bible, including how and when terms for certain parts of the female anatomy should be employed in the company of men, and so on. In doing so, like Brown, Evans uses 'grownup' words to talk about things like (gasp!) vaginas.

Her book caused a scandal, despite the fact that 'penis' was often referred to in Christian literature without the same visceral response. One line of thought was that this was because the folks with penises were likely to be the ones making the rules, as has been the case since time immemorial. Without labouring on the obvious, the subjugation of women to a lesser role than that of man was and probably still is evident in religious faiths.

(Oh, and do I need to mention *The Handmaid's Tale* by Margaret Atwood?)

But I'm not here to debate religion; rather, I want to bring to your attention this modern phenomenon.

THE UGLY SIDE OF VAGINAGATE

Vaginagate continues to rear its ugly head in many male-dominated organisations. For example, I know of one organisation (which I will not mention by name), where women remain a significant minority, and where its male members have long resisted the movement of women into their domain — a domain built on a fine history of traditions, professionalism and skill, but male none the less.

A male colleague of mine, a veteran of this organisation, was relaying to me a conversation he had with another male colleague in relation to the promotion of a woman. He used 'vaginagate' to describe the reason the woman was selected for promotion.

Now, as a woman and a feminist, I have no problem calling vaginas vaginas, in context and where appropriate. But to refer to this woman's promotion as being a result of 'vaginagate' is offensive, derogatory and demoralising. Where is the evidence of a lack of merit in the decision to promote her?

I actually thought that in 2019 we were past thinking that women were just being promoted or selected for attractive positions, promotions and opportunities solely because they were women. (That gets me onto another important issue relating to quotas and merit, but I'll talk about that in chapter 4.)

The deeper issue here is the prevailing attitude by men, and some women, about attempts by organisations to increase diversity and improve gender balance. They seem to think that gender equality means affirmative action for women and less of the 'equality pie' for men. More rights for women don't mean fewer rights for men — it's not pie! What is it about women's progression that makes them feel so threatened?

Maybe they're worried their own incompetence will be exposed. Or maybe the woman was just the best person for the job, promotion or opportunity.

In August 2013, after I had returned from Afghanistan as a gender adviser to NATO, I was appointed into a position created for me, with temporary promotion to Captain, to lead the implementation of the Australian Government National Action Plan on Women, Peace and Security 2012–2018. This plan outlined the way in which Australia would respond to the impact of conflict on women and children and how our national security agencies could implement a gender perspective across their national institutions and operations.

This was an extraordinary opportunity. I worked directly for the Chief of Defence Force (CDF). At this time, the position was held by Air Chief Marshal Mark Binskin, an amazing leader, and a pilot who had served firstly in the Navy and then the Air Force. And a man with whom I often crossed paths on motorcycle rides.

I was given privileged liaison authority with the Chiefs of Service. I was being trusted to develop an implementation plan, get stake-holder buy-in, and lead the whole-of-Defence response to the Plan. It was a high-profile role that exposed me to other government agencies, non-government organisations, academics and other civil-ian interest groups. I had to speak, run workshops, conduct training, attend meetings and conferences, and travel extensively overseas for the three-year duration of this posting.

And I was selected by the CDF to do this because I was the only Australian military member with the requisite skills, expertise and experience in the UN/NATO women, peace and security agenda.

I had completed all the relevant UN and NATO training. I had deployed operationally as a gender adviser (the first Australian military officer to do so). I had built an extensive network of NATO and UN member states personnel working on the same issue. I was qualified and competent, and clearly the Chief trusted me.

Let me repeat: I was the only and best person for this role. The evidence was there.

But then I heard the whispers. *She only got the job because she was a woman.* What the hell? The only basis for this assumption was that I was actually a woman.

Well, that was 2013. But to again hear in 2019 that 'vaginagate' is alive and well is so disappointing. That men say it, and women have to hear it, is a discredit to that particular organisation I mentioned earlier, and the profession as a whole.

In another example, a Norwegian Navy frigate, KNM *Helge Insgtad*, collided with a tanker in 2018, and four out of the five navigators on the frigate were women. Reporting on the incident, a male Norwegian journalist implied that the accident occurred as a result of human (that is, female) error.

He went on to suggest that the mandatory inclusion of women on a quota arrangement and with different requirements (which has been refuted by senior Navy personnel), had had an effect on the professional standards of the Norwegian armed forces. He then went even further to explain that the Navy's reticence to give out the details of the incident was evidence of a reluctance to draw attention to the gender of those who were at the helm at the time.

I know—journalists don't always have all the facts at hand. But that he would make such statements in the absence of evidence to support his contentions is itself evidence of 'vaginagate.'

Back at home in Australia, as I mention in the previous chapter, a 2012 review conducted by Elizabeth Broderick (former Australian Sex Discrimination Commissioner) into the treatment of women in the ADF[1] identified some 'deep and system contradictions' in the organisational culture of the ADF.

---

1   Broderick, Elizabeth. 2012. *Review into the Treatment of Women in the Australian Defence Force*. https://defence.humanrights.gov.au/sites/default/files/adf-complete.pdf

She identified that, on one hand, the organisation displayed an overwhelming (cultural) 'mantra' to 'treat everyone the same' or 'identically' (everyone wears the same uniform, for example, and is assessed on performance and promoted on merit). On the other hand, however, Broderick also identified aspects of ADF life and operations that set women apart — for example, different requirements regarding physical fitness, their ability to come in from field exercises to take showers and separated living quarters mean that women are sometimes seen as having special privileges.

In her report, Broderick said,

Certainly, there are circumstances where it is appropriate to treat men and women identically, such as where any significant gender differences are not relevant and where a 'level playing field' already exists. This must be balanced with circumstances where identical treatment will lead to inequality; such as when existing policies and practices are assumed to be neutral but in fact are embedded in a 'male norm'. [2]

There was definite evidence that some women preferred to blend into the masculine landscape, to be seen as one of the boys because the ADF was 'a man's world'. But she also discovered an equally strong view among some members that women generally have it easier than men in terms of their careers. In her report, she quoted one member as saying, 'The majority of females I reckon get it easy … If they request something and two people put their paperwork in, generally females would probably get it first.'

Again, no evidence substantiated this claim or opinion of the member quoted. It was just based on their misconceptions (or furphies as we say in the military) about how women are treated by the organisation and their equal or unequal access to opportunities, resources and promotions.

Interestingly, the Broderick Review also identified the strong resistance to targets or quotas — with the notion of differential treatment supposedly flying in the face of 'equality' as it's understood in the ADF, and members believing that equality would be achieved through identical treatment (which I'll talk more about in chapter 4).

---

2   Ibid, p. 2.

The Review highlighted that members believed quotas and merit were mutually exclusive and would undermine their achievements thus far. Another member was quoted in Broderick's report as saying:

> [For] the people that have worked so long for twenty years to be thought of as equal and then when you finally get promoted, they'll say you only got it because you're a female. Ruins everything we've done. Horrible, horrible thought.

And yet it is happening. Happening even with that level of 'equality' or 'merit' applied to the promotions or selections system. 'Vaginagate' is real.

And so, it seems that women cannot win. 'Vaginagate' wins—but not if we fight back.

MY TOP 5 TIPS

1. Some women and men seem to think that gender equality means affirmative action for women and less of the 'equality pie' for men. More rights for women don't mean fewer rights for men — it's not pie!

2. An organisation may have an overwhelming (cultural) 'mantra' to 'treat everyone the same' or 'identically', but often aspects of that organisation set women apart.

3. Some women prefer to blend into the masculine landscape, to be seen as 'one of the boys' because their organisation or workplace is 'a man's world'. Is this you?

4. People often hold strong views that, in cases of cultural reform focused on improving women's participation, women have it easier than men. What they are really saying is that women get ahead without merit because of this. What is the evidence of this?

5. Many women and men believe that quotas and merit are mutually exclusive and their application in the workplace would undermine their achievements. 'Vaginagate' is real!

Three

Where are the role models?

If you want something said, ask a man;
if you want something done, ask a woman.

Margaret Thatcher

How marvellous that Margaret Thatcher, the renowned 'Iron Lady' and ex-prime minister of the UK coined the phrase in the preceding quote. She was the longest-serving British prime minister of the 20th century (serving from 1979 to 1990) and the first woman to hold that office.

It was a Soviet journalist who dubbed her the 'Iron Lady', a nickname that became associated with her uncompromising politics and leadership style.

Whatever side of politics you are on, you have to be in awe of a woman who achieved so much. She clearly had a leadership style that was popular, and which saw her re-elected twice during her tenure. She was well educated (Oxford, no less) and served her entire career as a politician. She demonstrated, in my view, determination, tenacity and true grit in her rise to the prime ministerial role.

Something we could all learn from.

Okay, so the UK has only had one more female prime minister since (Theresa May), but Margaret was the first and she was well and truly prepared to be the first, to be a role model for female politicians, both in her homeland and around the world.

How prepared and willing are we women to still be role models?

I see so many Australian women in male-dominated professions who, once they've reached the top, the first in a particular role, still want to be 'beige'. They still don't want to be seen as different from their male colleagues, usually for fear of been judged as achieving their position without merit.

In June 2019, at a women's leadership program run by long-term friend and colleague Avril Henry, I was privileged to hear Wendy McCarthy, AO, speak about her very long career and ground-breaking achievements for women. She has spent a lifetime challenging the status quo, taking opportunities presented to her (even when she didn't yet know how to do what the opportunity involved), and making her mark as a feminist. She really has been on the frontline of so much social change from which women today are benefitting.

In the area of women in male-dominated professions, forging careers within that masculine construct and fearing the fanfare that might be attached to their 'first', McCarthy said, the 'fear of pushing themselves forward is still a cultural imprint today'. She was concerned that women today might 'squander the fruits of feminism for fear of speaking out'.

Conversely, I see posts on social media all the time celebrating women's achievements in foreign militaries, police forces, in peace-keeping, in STEM (science, technology, engineering and mathematics) occupations, and in mining.

But what has happened to the role models? Well, my contemporaries and I, who in the uncertain days of change in the 1990s and 2000s, broke down systemic barriers and became the 'firsts' in many areas, are still around. But we still need role models today in new and emerging areas.

Our workplaces (and professions) are rapidly evolving and women have many opportunities to step up and be the 'first'. And where this happens, we should still make a point of acknowledging and celebrating that achievement, so other women can see that it can be done.

Of course, some women and men argue that women's 'firsts' should just be treated as 'business as usual' and the 'norm', in order to normalise it. They ask why women's achievements should be celebrated more than men's. That argument would work if the 'norm' was a more gender-balanced organisation, where the pools from which selections are made have increased numbers of women to even the level of diversity, where diversity is genuinely at the core of all decisions and where, strategically, the organisation was doing everything within its power to increase women's participation. Gender nirvana!

In her speech that day in June 2019, Ms McCarthy also challenged us to consider our mindset around women's leadership and in women being role models, by asserting that women may potentially, in their desire to remain 'beige' and be the same as the person (male) before them, be limiting their aspirations. McCarthy argued this was a sign of accepting the 'norm' rather than fighting to expand it. American writer and psychologist Timothy Leary said something similar: 'Women who seek to be equal with men lack ambition.'

McCarthy suggested that women stop trying to be 'just as good as the men' and aspire to increasing opportunities for women and diversity.

What is stopping you? Are you afraid that you and your leadership style will be judged by your peers?

FEMININE LEADERSHIP

All you need is the compassion of the heart.
Women know this because peace is implicit in women.
You put boys together, they make war.
You put women together, they make peace.
Women are the leaders of the future.

Dalai Lama, 2019

I've always felt like a woman. I look like one, too. Admittedly, when I joined the Navy, I felt quite comfortable in the uniform of white dress, gloves, pantyhose, lace-up shoes and handbag (much like the school uniform of Hornsby Girls High School I'd just moved on from) and a hat (a tricorne style based on that worn by Napoleon Bonaparte and many other mariners in the 18th and early 19th century). It wasn't a stretch!

I didn't wear makeup then. I suppose when you're 19 years old, with sun-kissed hair and tanned skin (I wonder where that girl is now!) you don't have to. When I appeared before a panel for promotion to sub-lieutenant in 1983, I was scolded by the same senior female officer I'd encountered in my earlier selection board (mentioned in the preface) — this time for not wearing makeup and tying my shoelaces the wrong way.

Good lord. And to think I thought perhaps my potential for leadership, my performance and my achievements might actually bear some weight. Well, I passed the board, and the senior officer's comments didn't make me wear makeup.

That said, I always felt like I led like a woman. And I mean this in a way that echoes the sentiment put forward by Clementine Ford in *Fight Like a Girl*, a marvellous book that calls out the ways in which girls and women are hurt and held back by those who feel threatened by feminism or gender equality. She exposes how unequal the world continues to be.

Phrases like 'you throw like a girl' or 'you run like a girl', usually said to men as an insult to their masculinity, only serve to undermine women and their capabilities. Or even their untapped potential!

What I love about Ford's message is the fact that doing anything like a girl is exactly that, and nothing to be ashamed of or something that needs to change. You should fight like a girl, run like a girl, swim like a girl, and so on. Another message is for girls and women to raise their voices, raise their courage, and raise the flag (for feminism and equality).

Now I know Ford (like Thatcher) is controversial, and you either love her or hate her. But her book title is an overt message to those who continue to use gendered language to describe (and dismiss) women's abilities or achievements.

I love how this message is now being used by others to subtly ask, what is wrong with doing it the way a woman does? Take the story of Michelle Payne, who, in 2015, became the first female jockey to win Australia's Melbourne Cup. A movie about her and 'her-storical' win, *Ride Like a Girl*, was released in 2019. The movie depicts her and her family's story, and the ups, downs, success and struggles she faced in her journey to become a champion jockey within a very male-dominated sport.

In an interview with an Australian magazine in October 2019, Michelle was quoted as saying, 'I was pretty much told I couldn't do it. He [her dad] always used to say to us that the girls were as good as the boys, and to seize the opportunity.' While, as already mentioned, I don't subscribe to the notion or language that women have to be 'as good as the men'—because this book is all about achieving success by being yourself—I do agree that women's achievements are about seizing opportunities.

Similarly, the film's director Rachel Griffiths, a well-known Australian actor, was quoted as saying, 'It's a "you can't be what you can't see" film, and I think that girls … will feel inspired seeing a woman succeed in a male-dominated industry.'

And, of course, as a role model, Michelle will do exactly that. But, for herself, she had to be what she *couldn't* see because no woman was before her. She was a girl, she rode her best, and she won ahead of her male peers. She rode like a girl! And she was proud of being a woman who had achieved this milestone.

I think Michelle exhibited quiet feminine leadership. She wasn't in your face about it, but she also didn't hide behind 'gender equality', and she certainly wasn't 'beige'.

WHAT TYPE OF LEADERSHIP DO YOU EXHIBIT?

Again, I know you may find yourself defaulting to the 'I'm just the same as the men' model of leadership. I know some of you have felt you needed to do this to be accepted, to survive.

But what if you used your femininity in leadership in a way that benefits other women?

In 'The four types of female leadership', published in *HR Magazine* UK, authors Steve Tappin and Ana Marinovic argue four types of feminine leadership are seen. They are:

- *Female pioneers:* These women 'tend to act more in the manner of alpha male leaders' and have had to deal with being seen as the 'token women' throughout their careers. According to Tappin and Marinovic, their leadership style is 'forthright and no-nonsense, because this is what has been proven to make a difference in the male-dominated boys clubs'. These pioneering women have left a strong foothold in male-dominated corporate organisations for others to step up. An example Tappin and Marinovic cite is Meg Whitman, former CEO of Hewlett Packard and current CEO of mobile video platform Quibi.

- *Feminine leaders:* These women have more confidence to bring 'feminine' qualities to work, such as being more caring and communicative, better listeners and more collaborative. An example is Carolyn McCall, former CEO of EasyJet and now CEO of ITV in the UK.

- *The integrated woman:* These women have become strong leaders and have gained influence 'through their ambition and drive to succeed'. Tappin and Marinovic argue these women have 'generally integrated their life experiences and developed leadership philosophies that they use as a guiding compass'. Work is less separated from the home, and they are 'very good at collaborating, empowering, connecting and co-creating with both men and women'. An example is Lindsay Pattison, CEO of Maxus and chief transformation officer for media investment conglomerate GroupM.

- *Women of inspiration:* These women display characteristics from the three other leadership types and 'are driven by a higher purpose, are often globally recognised, and have broken free from male-dominated leadership constraints. They've started a chain of women of inspiration from the top'. Examples Tappin and Marinovic offer are Arianna Huffington, Malala Yousafzai, and Mary Barra.

For more on Tappin and Marinovic's take on the four types of female leaders, go to www.hrmagazine.co.uk/article-details/the-four-types-of-female-leadership.

I like to think I'm a blend of the 'integrated woman and a 'woman of inspiration'. I say this because I have always tried to lead like a woman, and never tried to be something I wasn't—a man.

It was important to me that I brought my own authentic personal qualities to any and all situations I faced. I wanted my people to feel valued, supported and nurtured. That didn't mean I couldn't take charge or mete out discipline when it was required. It just meant I led naturally—to me.

I remember in 1984 giving a young sailor feedback on his annual performance report. It wasn't pretty. His report reflected an inferior performance. Although he knew this, he had lost heart in his current occupation as a steward (similar to a waiter) because he wanted to become a Navy diver (equivalent to US Navy Seals) and his application had been rejected. An inferior report can lead to termination of service. He cried. I did feel a bit awkward, having a young man in my office crying (there goes the gendered stereotypes that men don't cry!).

But we talked, and talked, and talked. He came around to the realisation that, for the moment, he was stuck doing what he was doing. Quietly, he picked up his game. Indeed, he starting doing so well, he was selected to be the Commanding Officer's valet. His outstanding performance in this role led to the award of a commendation from the commanding officer. I was quietly proud of what he had achieved and I like to think I helped him see what he could be.

Feminine leadership? It's a good thing. I don't know if the process and outcome would have been different if I had been a man. Probably, in 1984, that would have been the case. Probably, that sailor would have been kicked out of the Navy.

What I will say is don't be afraid to go on a journey to work through your authentic personal leadership style, so you can unshackle yourself from the masculine construct and harness those best qualities of yourself—feminine or otherwise!

Take a deep dive into yourself, discover your purpose and passion, and let this drive your leadership.

MY TOP 5 TIPS

1. Our workplaces (and professions) are rapidly evolving and women have many opportunities to step up and be the 'first'. And where this happens, we should still make a point of acknowledging and celebrating that achievement, so other women can see that it can be done.

2. Consider your mindset around women's leadership and in women being role models. In a desire to remain 'beige' or 'unseen' in male-dominated workplaces, do some women have limited aspirations to be the same as the person (a male) before them?

3. Stop trying to be 'just as good as the men' — you already are and have nothing to prove — and aspire to increasing opportunities for women and diversity.

4. Girls and women can be hurt and held back by those who feel threatened by feminism or gender equality. Be like Clementine Ford and Michelle Payne. Fight like a girl, run like a girl, swim like a girl, and so on. Don't be afraid to raise your voice, raise your courage, and raise the flag (for feminism and equality).

5. Think about your femininity in leadership. How do you use it to benefit other women? Do for them what you would do for yourself!

Four

Why is the 'gender boat' still sailing?

I think women are foolish to pretend they are equal to men;
they are far superior and always have been.

William Golding, author of *Lord of the Flies*

Well, why the 'gender boat' is still sailing is a good question. In the previous chapter, I mention hearing Wendy McCarthy speak at a leadership seminar run by Avril Henry, where McCarthy reflected on her legacy and that of her feminist peers. She said, 'It's not where we would like it to be. Today, we're just having re-runs of the same old conversations.'

I know many of my colleagues in male-dominated professions wonder why we keep talking about gender when really, we wear the same uniform, we get paid (in the Australian military at least) the same for the same work, and we are selected for promotion on 'merit' (I'll talk more about that later in the chapter). But gender equality doesn't necessarily equate to better balance or equitable treatment.

One problem is we get the various gender terms mixed up when we are talking about increasing women's participation and representation and what is needed in terms of organisational approaches to get that balance. But let's look at that idea of 'balance' first. Why do we want or need balance?

FINDING BALANCE

For a start, aiming for a better gender balance in organisations is a primary tool to achieve gender equality.

Simply put, gender balance is defined, by the European Institute of Gender Equality, as the 'equal participation of women and men in all areas of work, projects or programs.'

In some organisations, such as Wesfarmers (a leading Australian listed company), gender balance is achieved through strategies to ensure a minimum of 40 per cent of either gender (much like the Australian Government's approach to women on boards, which I touch on later in this chapter). This is because they believe that gender-balanced businesses enable them to better deliver on their objective of satisfactory returns to stakeholders.

Indeed, in 2019, Wesfarmers has demonstrated great results. The leadership team comprises 45 per cent women, and the total workforce comprises 58 per cent women. They acknowledge they have further work to do to improve that balance in both senior executive positions (currently 27 per cent women) and management and professional roles (36 per cent women).

Interestingly, Wesfarmers Group Managing Director is part of Elizabeth Broderick's Male Champions of Change (MCC)[1] in making a personal commitment to take action to advance gender equality.

The Australian military, with historically low levels of participation of women (despite women comprising 52 per cent of the population), has set 'gender balance' targets to be achieved by 2023; these are 25 per cent for Navy and Air Force and 15 per cent for Army. While these still fall short of the now commonly accepted standard of 40 per cent across organisations and boards, they are based on previous and current recruiting trends and expectations, and it is expected that these targets will be achieved.

This is a great step forward in recognising the value that women bring to that profession and organisational outcomes, and in seeking to improve greater equality for both women and men.

---

1   Male Champions of Change was created by Elizabeth Broderick during her tenure as Australia's Sex Discrimination Commissioner to engage male leaders to advocate for and act to advance gender equality. Find out more at malechampionsofchange.com.

EQUALITY VERSUS EQUITY

What is gender equality? Also known as sexual equality or equality of the sexes, it's generally accepted as the state of equal ease of access to resources and opportunities regardless of gender, including economic participation and decision-making, and the state of valuing different behaviours, aspirations and needs equally, regardless of gender.

Gaining equality does not mean that women and men will become the same but that women's and men's rights, responsibilities and opportunities will not depend on whether they are born male or female. Gender equality implies that the interests, needs and priorities of both women and men are taken into consideration, recognising the diversity of different groups of women and men.

Broadly, the aim of gender equality in the workplace is to achieve equal opportunities and outcomes for women and men, but not necessarily outcomes that are exactly the same for all. The Workplace Gender Equality Agency, the Australian Government statutory agency charged with promoting and improving gender equality in Australian workplaces[2], says that achieving equality requires:

- workplaces to provide equal pay for work of equal or comparable value

- removal of barriers to the full and equal participation of women in the workforce

- access to all occupations and industries, including leadership roles, regardless of gender

- elimination of discrimination on the basis of gender, particularly in relation to family and caring responsibilities.

So, we know this is what we are after.

But the problem is that (lay) people assume that equality means treating everyone the same. If this was the case, as shown in the following popular infographic, everyone would be starting from the same point, regardless of their differences. The following infographic

---

2   Created by the *Workplace Gender Equality Act 2012*.

from the Interaction Institute for Social Change[3] shows that, even when the three boys have an equal-sized box, the differences in their height mean they don't all get to see the game!

EQUALITY   EQUITY

Equality promotes fairness and justice by giving everyone the same thing. But this can only work if everyone is starting from the same place.

Equity, on the other hand, is about fairness, and ensuring people get access to the same opportunities. Sometimes our differences and/or history can create barriers to participation, so we must first ensure equity before we can enjoy equality.

If everyone is different, different responses or approaches are required.

We haven't achieved equality just by putting women into the same uniform, albeit adjusted for female figures, as men. We haven't achieved equality by paying everyone the same based on rank and occupation.

3   Reproduced by permission from the Interaction Institute for Social Change; artist: Angus Maguire.

Because differences and history, especially in organisations such as the armed forces and police, have precluded women from accessing resources and opportunities equally. In the Australian military, for example, the government only lifted the gender restrictions on combat-related roles in the early 1990s and on combat roles in 2011.

While participation levels of women in these roles have increased slightly, the benefits of such a step is yet to be fully realised. Because male-dominated organisations often build their workforce from within, and the inherent hierarchical structure is generally based on traditional benchmarks, women are, in 2019, still behind the curveball. They didn't start on an even playing field, and the continued low numbers in particular professions continues to marginalise the role that women can play overall.

A good example I can share comes from the Navy. As I've mentioned, I joined the Navy in 1981 as what is now known as a maritime logistics officer and back then, as I've also mentioned, women didn't serve at sea or deploy. So, I was posted to numerous logistics roles as a junior officer at shore bases, admittedly following a similar career path to men. Did this make me equal? No, because the men also had postings to ships, which, you know, is exactly what we want Navy people to do. That's the Navy's *raison d'être*. And creating a career based on sea service was what was required in order to get promoted.

When I first joined, I don't think I (or the few women colleagues I had) really thought about what was ahead for us in light of not being able to serve at sea. After the WRANS was disbanded in 1984 and women were amalgamated into the RAN, our performance—and potential—was assessed against our male colleagues. So not really an even playing field, or an even starting point.

Then in the early 1990s as the restrictions on combat-related roles were lifted, women started to post to ships. Another female colleague of mine, Siobhan (in fact, we joined the Navy together), and I were posted, as Lieutenant Commanders, to our ships in 1996 as the senior maritime logistics officers, without the added benefits of previous sea service that held our male colleagues in good stead for an officer-in-charge position.

Indeed, we had been told if we wanted to get promoted to the next rank (commander), we had to go to sea, but were offered no guarantee that our performance in one sea posting would be adequate to assess our future potential.

So, my generation didn't get an even playing field, and I'm sure no one would know the extent to which this unevenness impacted women at the time. Of course, for female maritime logistic officers now, and since the 1990s, their entire career has been on par with the men.

Australia's *Sex Discrimination Act 1984* made discrimination 'on the basis of sex' (and you gotta love the story of Ruth Bader Ginsburg, later US Supreme Court judge, who made her-story in the 1970s with her winning cases on gender discrimination) and sexual harassment, in various parts of public life, illegal. (This is what led the Navy to move its women into the RAN.) Wider than that, the Act has, of course, helped advance gender equality, but because of the historical context and differences that have been in place for women across many organisations, gender equality remains problematic. To illustrate this, statistics produced by the Australian Human Rights Commission (AHRC) in 2018 demonstrate that women and girls continue to experience inequality and discrimination in the workplace, which limits choices and opportunities available to them.

According to the AHRC, the barriers to gender equality include:

- The Australian workforce is highly segregated by gender, and female-dominated industries such as aged care, childcare and health and community services have been historically undervalued. Australian women are over-represented as part-time workers in low-paid industries and in insecure work, and continue to be underrepresented in leadership roles in the private and public sectors.

- More than half of women aged 18 or older have experienced sexual harassment in their lifetime.

- On average, women spend 64 per cent of their working week performing unpaid care work. They spend almost twice as many hours performing such work each week compared to men.

- In 2015–2016, the average Australian woman was reaching retirement with an average of $113,660 less superannuation than the average male. As a result, women are more likely to experience poverty in their retirement years and be far more reliant on the Age Pension.

- More than one in three Australian women has experienced physical or sexual violence in her lifetime and one in two has experienced sexual harassment.

- One in five Australian women has experienced violence from a partner since the age of 15, with violence against women and their children estimated to have cost the Australian economy $22 billion in 2015–16.

(To access an infographic summarising these statistics and others, go to www.humanrights.gov.au/our-work/education/face-facts-gender-equality-2018.)

On the face of it, many men and women in male-dominated professions think they have equality, when in fact they don't.

Because women are still playing catch-up.

Because the uneven playing field has not been evened out.

SAMENESS

Talking about even playing fields leads me to the notion of 'sameness'. In terms of equality, this means treating everyone the same. From a sameness approach, the simplest way to remedy the history of discrimination against women in the military is to assert that sex difference is irrelevant to military service and lift all bans on women serving, which in Australia occurred fully by 2011.

If enlistment previously required that one had to be an 18-year-old male meeting certain physical requirements (such as no major disabilities, good vision and ability to demonstrate a certain level of strength), a sameness approach would mean we could just take 'male' out of the list of requirements. The advantage of this approach is that, on the face of things, it does appear to achieve formal equality: men and women receive the same treatment.

The disadvantage is that this approach ignores the fact that, on average, men as a group and women as a group do have somewhat different physical characteristics and capacities. The physical requirements in place for enlistment were based on male bodies, so leaving them unchanged may continue to discriminate against women.

I hear all the time from my military colleagues that men and women should do the same annual physical fitness test 'as a measure of equality'. However, they all seem to ascribe to the notion that as women were introduced later, equality means having the women complete the test that was in place historically for men.

No one seems to be calling for new standards to be set based on what was appropriate for men and women together, if this is at all possible to achieve. If men and women get fit at different rates and levels based on physiology and anatomy, it seems simple enough to me — although I'm no expert in this area — that men and women can be equally fit enough to qualify for a role but that the requirements to demonstrate this can still be different. Am I Robinson Crusoe in thinking this?

In the US, the different services of the military have slightly different physical fitness test requirements for women and men and each age group. An American academic, Brian Schilling, Chair of Kinesiology and Nutrition Sciences at the University of Nevada, Las Vegas, has said:

> It would be too difficult to determine a single physical standard for men and women — and most likely, such a standard would be too difficult for women to reach … It is biologically correct to say that 'physically fit' for a woman is different to 'physically fit' for a man … this is based on sex differences in body composition, muscular strength, muscular endurance … etc. Both the PFT and the CFT are meant to measure a Marine's overall fitness, not how ready they are for combat.

This approach acknowledges some physical differences between men and women, on average, and adjusts the physical fitness test requirements to accommodate those differences. The adjustments are slight, so the approach also recognises the fact that women can achieve roughly comparable levels of fitness and strength to men.

In the quote, Schilling makes the point that while the standards are different, they result in a comparable level of fitness. This point seems to be lost on proponents of 'equal' or 'gender-neutral' (I'll talk about this idea of gender blindness shortly) physical tests as a measure of equality between the sexes, who claim that any changes to acknowledge the differences result in a lowering of fitness standards.

The debate on this issue continues.

This 'sameness' approach also ignores relevant differences in another way. Without addressing the fact that some professions have been male historically, simply changing the sex requirement fails to address the fact of cultural differences.

Indeed, implementing this policy change in isolation from other supplementary educational changes ignores the long historical development of a culture of masculinity (discussed in chapter 1). This is what has happened in some modern militaries—as I've mentioned previously, for example, when women started being posted on ships in the 1990s, we didn't take into account nor anticipate the resistance from some men—and their wives!

Even when women are 'added to the pot', long-entrenched patterns of masculine socialisation can remain unchanged, including such beliefs that women do not belong in the military, as can attitudes or habits of treating women as sexual objects. The problem of sexual harassment still remains an issue in modern militaries, as it does in police, as evidenced by Elizabeth Broderick's report on the NSW Police (refer to chapter 1), and as indicated in the AHRC statistics in the previous section in this chapter.

These persisting attitudes may reduce or compromise the numbers of women who attempt to enlist in male-dominated professions such as the armed forces (along with many others). This is an example of how, on its own, a 'sameness' or 'formal equality' approach to discrimination fails to address the ways that real differences (either biological or sociocultural) significantly affect the presence of women.

So why do we want or need gender diversity?

Why do we want to create a better balance between the genders in traditionally male-dominated professions? Why do we want women to have more equitable or fairer representation in their workplace?

Well, in short, the business case for greater gender diversity has been made and can be summarised as follows:

- Management with greater gender diversity tends to perform better than that dominated by one gender.

- Gender diversity brings multiple benefits to companies, including an overall increase in business performance, number of customers, revenues and profits.

- By promoting gender diversity, companies are also more likely to attract more diverse people.

- Studies show that higher diversity in the workforce can be expected to bring higher financial returns.

- Gender diversity improves reputation and organisational image.

- A gender-diverse workforce enables better problem-solving, because men and women have different viewpoints, ideas and market insights.

- Hiring a gender-diverse workforce allows the company to serve an increasingly diverse customer base.

The preceding points are not an exhaustive list.

In operational professions, such as the military or police, an increased presence of women can bring additional benefits such as reducing sexual harassment (because having more women around the workplace becomes more normal, with those present less likely to be singled out). On operational deployments, having both women and men deployed creates more effective operational outcomes, because they can both use their different backgrounds and experiences to tap into the different social and cultural needs of the local community.

When I was in Afghanistan in 2013, serving as a gender adviser to NATO in the International Security Assistance Force Joint Command, my role was to ensure gender mainstreaming in all of the command's lines of operations, including counterinsurgency, stabilisation and security assistance operations. This meant delivering the commander's (and NATO's) gender policy across all aspects of the command's operations, providing advice and guidance to senior leadership on all matters relating to gender (as it applied to the Afghan security sector and general population), and providing training and education to all NATO personnel on the importance of gender perspective to human security.

As part of this, I was able to meet with a group of policewomen in the Kabul City Police Station. This was organised for me by (then) Major General Jody Osterman, USMC, the Deputy Chief of Staff (Operations). The NATO mission at that time was focused on counter-insurgency activities, but a separate mandate included assisting the Afghan security forces with recruiting more women and improving their rights and equality. The women I met were varied in age, backgrounds and marital and family status. Some were my age and quite senior in rank; they had been police officers before the Taliban came to power and prevented them from exercising their rights to work in public. Some were young mothers; some were widows supporting families. Their circumstances affected me in so many ways.

We sat and nattered for about two hours, through interpreters of course, but it was an amazing opportunity to learn so much about their lives, their professional prospects, and their desire to contribute to the rebuilding of Afghanistan. This was a real privilege.

In this conversation, we talked about issues that were particular to their experience as women—the lack of childcare, for example, ill-fitting uniforms, lack of choice and opportunities, sexual harassment, lower conditions of service, inadequate facilities such as change rooms, judgement by their families and neighbours for working with men ... and potentially risking their lives everyday travelling to and from work. They were often targeted by insurgents and even family members and some, along with other high-profile, public women, were murdered. It really put gender equality into perspective.

I was able to use this information to help inform some of NATO's efforts to support the Afghan government in increasing women's participation in the Afghan army and police. They also saw the imperative for having female officers in their operational forces to conduct searches of women, support female victims of crime, particularly harassment and violence, and look after women and children during counter-insurgency raids.

But had I been a male gender adviser, I simply would not have been able to have this conversation and gain these insights. This small example of 'gender perspective' demonstrated the importance of, and need for, a balance in deployed units.

Not rocket science, people!

Gender perspective versus gender blindness

Let's move onto gender perspective and gender blindness.

Gender perspective is a term commonly used by those in militaries and police forces around the world in their approaches when conducting operations or peacekeeping missions, and it has grown in its importance and application over the past ten years.

The term has a long history, and you can search it online to learn more, but it initially arose as an element of the first UN Security Council Resolution 1325 on Women, Peace and Security, adopted in 2000. This resolution and another eight in the following years have been implemented by over eighty UN member states, including Australia, through the development of national action plans. Among other things, these resolutions require various national security agencies in Australia to take a gender perspective in the planning and execution of all operations and exercises.

Okay, great. But what does it mean? Well, as it sounds, having a gender perspective means considering gender-based differences between women and men, as reflected in their social roles and interactions, in the distribution of power and access to resources (this is the NATO definition). Simply, this means taking gender differences into account when making decisions that affect women and men.

It really is common sense when you think that our armed forces and police deploy to countries that have significant cultural, religious and social differences that require us to be able to assist in a sensitive and respectful way.

Conversely, being gender blind is disregarding these differences as a significant factor influencing interactions between people — getting back to the 'sameness' approach, in other words. The problem with this is that gender blindness can downplay the existence of real gender differences, which can reinforce existing gender inequality.

So, we've come a full circle, and I hope this helps explain a little more about why we do or don't take gender into account, and the effects of either approach. Let's move on to how acknowledging differences in the playing field for women can lead to charges of tokenism (and how this then runs into the debate of quotas versus merit).

TOKENISM

Along with wanting to be seen as 'equal' to men (discussed in chapter 1) some women also don't want to be noticed for fear of being described as the 'token woman', with the inherent belief that being seen as such means they did not get where they are on merit, or that their success is more to do with appearances than aptitude. And yet for generations of women before us, women were in 'token' numbers as we slowly challenged barriers to participation, irrespective of the notion of merit, substance or otherwise. Somebody had to do it!

But as I talk about, and firmly believe in, gender perspective, so should we focus on the value that even the 'token' woman can bring to the workplace. What happens when a woman's ideas are actually heard and enacted by her male colleagues?

Well, according to a 2019 study by a collective of US universities and University of Melbourne[4], complex tasks are performed more expeditiously and effectively when token women's voices are included. The authors of the study, which used US military teams, also argue that just adding a woman isn't enough, and that other factors such as leadership also play an important role and are essential.

---

4   Farh, Chrystal I.C, Oh, Jo K, Yu, Andrew, Lee, Stephanie M, and King, Danielle D, 2019. 'Token female voice enactment in traditionally male-dominated teams: Facilitating conditions and consequences for performance'. Published in *Academy of Management Journal*, In-Press. Accessed on 20 August 2019 at https://journals.aom.org/doi/10.5465/amj.2017.0778.

This is not dissimilar to the plethora of feminist research in my field of expertise—women, peace and security—which argues that gender perspective in militaries creates more effective operational outcomes. Robert Egnell, a world-renowned gender expert, friend and colleague, and now the Vice Chancellor of the Swedish Defence University, argues that adding a gender perspective has the potential to transform the traditional military paradigm by including and creating an increased understanding of the importance of non-traditional security issues.[5]

The synergies here underline the importance of women's inclusion in not just the military, but also any workplace, and particularly those that are male dominated. The 2019 study just mentioned, for example, found that all-male teams tended to keep trying the same solution without effect, but that complex tasks benefitted from the introduction of new and novel ideas by the token minority.

So, as long as the token woman's voice can be heard, outcomes will be better. My point is, don't be afraid to be that token woman—unless, of course, you want to be 'beige'.

QUOTAS, TARGETS AND MERIT

While we're on the subject of gender equality, let's tackle some big issues: quotas, targets and merit. All of these things are designed to improved women's participation in traditionally male-dominated occupations but all are very much debated, contested or misunderstood. The difference between quotas and targets is probably the least understood, as the average Joe Blow interprets them both as measures to advantage women over men—or, more specifically, to select incompetent women over more qualified, competent men.

On social media last year, I watched a video of two men discussing gender and diversity quotas in the workplace. The younger of the two commenced his argument against quotas by citing 'set standards' and being 'suitable for the job'. He also said, 'you want the best people out

---

5   Egnell, Robert. 'Gender perspectives and military effectiveness: Implementing UNSCR 1325 and the National Action Plan on Women, Peace and Security'. Published in PRISM 6, No.1.

there' and that political correctness was leading us to selecting people for the job on the basis of being 'more diverse instead of who's more qualified', or even to lowering the required standards.

Similarly, a friend quoted a senior official in a male-dominated sector as saying, 'I think the concept of quotas to get more women in [leadership] positions is a great disservice to them. It would compromise the position of all female [leaders] and leave [subordinate staff] with a view that their female [leader] only got the job due to a quota ahead of a better qualified man'.

The implication from both scenarios was clear, and quite offensive in my view: quotas equate to incompetence and, as they are generally deployed to increase women's representation, they allow incompetent women to be selected over 'better qualified men' and, ultimately, that the 'best people for the job' are not women.

Why do senior (male) leaders of organisations continue to perpetuate these unfounded myths at the risk of alienating their very talented, qualified and professional women? Why do women and men feel that any selection or promotion under a gender diversity quota demeans or diminishes their achievements, potential, abilities and qualifications, or that the selection of a woman based on gender inherently means she is less competent than a man? Why do people feel it's problematic to address gender inequality and imbalance in the workplace just by reversing the existing concept of 'quota' based on gender and race held by men for centuries? Are men afraid of being caught out on their mediocrity?

Well, what does a quota mean?

I like this definition of quota from the European Institute of Gender Equality:

Positive measurement instrument aimed at accelerating the achievement of gender-balanced participation and representation by establishing a defined proportion (percentage) or number of places or seats to be filled by, or allocated to, women and/or men, generally under certain rules or criteria.

Hmm, sounds like a special measure that can be employed to even up the playing field. Oh, did I state the obvious?

I know this stirs up emotions in so many women, who think quotas will demean their achievements, and in men, who think they will miss an opportunity or a 'piece of the pie' because it will be given to an incompetent woman.

In Victoria, the state government is in the process of delivering a Gender Equality Bill, recommending a 40:40:20 target—40 per cent women, 40 per cent men and 20 per cent flexible—for all senior management and executive roles in the public sector. This reflects the federal government's policy, implemented in 2016, where they committed to a gender diversity target of women holding 50 per cent of government board positions overall, and women and men each holding at least 40 per cent of positions at the individual board level.

A media report in late 2018 cited the acting chief executive officer of Victoria's leading women's advocacy group as saying,

> *My immediate feelings about quotas is that if you say you're against them then you're almost saying that there's been no women of merit for the past 100 years. People say, 'Well, you can get there on merit'. So, men have had merit throughout history, but women haven't been and still aren't as clever, talented and meritorious?*

I'll talk about merit shortly, but it's interesting that generally women and men dismiss quotas as being exclusive of merit and perpetuating the notion of incompetent women being selected over competent men for promotion in a system that has overlooked qualified women for decades.

Yet because of the historically masculine cultures of many male-dominated professions, the very dominance of one gender (male) led to a greater proportion of men in the very leadership roles that need gender balance as a business (or, in the military's case, operational effectiveness) necessity.

Thankfully, one senior female colleague in Defence, interviewed by Elizabeth Broderick in 2012 in her review into the treatment of women in the ADF, said,

> *Many will argue that they don't want to be promoted based on a quota, that they want to get there on merit. Well, quotas and merit are not mutually exclusive ideas. Well, we all need to get over it. The reality*

is that every woman who goes to the short list at a promotion board has merit anyway.

Targets are similarly dismissed as another measure to reduce men's participation, ostensibly at the risk of recruiting less competent women. Targets are also often accompanied by special measures, such as targeted recruiting for women, which help further whip up the frenzy (and myths) around competence and merit—let's look at that myth in particular.

The myth of merit

In 2016, Julie McKay, previous Executive Director of UN Women Australia, and at that time part-time Gender Adviser to the CDF, wrote an eloquent article for the Australian Institute of Company Directors, titled 'Addressing the merit myth'.

McKay wrote this article because in both her roles she faced the problem of 'merit' receiving the usual and standard response whenever she challenged organisations about women's participation and why they hadn't been promoted. What she aimed to do was unpack the subjective concept of 'merit' to understand its impact on perpetuating gender inequality.

In her article, McKay cited the well-known Heidi vs Howard study, which saw participants ranking the same résumé more favourably when Howard Roizen was the candidate rather than Heidi Roizen (each with exactly the same résumé). Participants acknowledged that Heidi was obviously well-accomplished and highly competent but were less likely to want to work with her or for her.

McKay went on to argue, 'Merit is some combination of past performance and future potential and is in large part a subjective measure.'

So, for the women and men shouting down quotas or targets as being exclusive of merit, in fact the traditional system in many male-dominated professions is a form of merit based on unconscious bias and unacknowledged quotas that perpetuate gender inequality.

The key to enabling special measures like quotas or targets to exist and enable greater participation by women is in the leadership of the organisation. Julie concluded her article by saying,

Leaders need to reshape the conversation we have about merit to ensure that women do not face a backlash when they are promoted, with claims that they only got there because they were women.

Overcoming the myth of merit requires leaders to step up and acknowledge that the current process is impacted by bias and that 'cultural fit' often disadvantages diverse candidates.

Another expert worth listening to is Catherine Fox, journalist and author of 7 *Myths About Women and Work.* According to Fox, merit is a subjective term that is really just 'smoke and mirrors', a 'self-reinforcing concept for those in charge'. Basically, when this occurs, like selects like. In corporate Australia this has resulted in men being 'nine times more meritorious than females as CEOs in the ASX 200'.

In other male-dominated professions, such as law, women make up to two-thirds of university graduates yet fill only one-in-10 senior counsel and Queen's counsel positions (according to the Law Council of Australia).

As Fox says, we often hear that 'he got it on merit', and that the perpetuation of this term is handy because 'it doesn't rock the boat … and perpetuates inertia'. In short, she says, the term 'merit' is an excuse used not to take action to address inequality.

And what about the predominance of men in most areas of leadership—in the corporate world, on boards, in politics and, up until 2019, even in the Australian honours list? Do we really believe that no competent, qualified and talented women are available to compete with men for these roles?

In her book, Fox quotes the work of Avivah Wittenberg-Cox, a UK-based consultant. In her blog Wittenberg-Cox wrote:

Most male managers I work with have no idea how male normed today's corporate cultures, management mindsets and policy processes still are. Many haven't given it a moment's thought … And most senior male executives have never (yet) left their male-dominated environments … They have rarely experienced the pleasure of being the only man in a roomful of women. When they do it usually has a profound impact—and they are very often amazed to discover how uncomfortable it is.

In the same blog, Wittenberg-Cox also highlights the dangers for women when they buy into these same ideas of merit. Women adopting male standards (to then be seen as having the same merit as men) create a negative cycle, where the role model they are providing means younger women are demotivated by these 'inauthentic, adaptive women'. According the Wittenberg-Cox, these women then 'quit (physically and intellectually), often citing "personal reasons" and then companies complain about retention.

Those women who do get promoted under this idea of merit are more likely to support it because the system worked for them. And then if one or two get through, we're back to vaginagate (refer to chapter 2)! Where's the merit in that?

MY TOP 5 TIPS

1. Gender equality, also known as sexual equality or equality of the sexes, is the state of equal ease of access to resources and opportunities, including economic participation and decision-making, and the state of valuing different behaviours, aspirations and needs equally, regardless of gender.

2. Equality promotes fairness and justice by giving everyone the same thing. But it can only work if everyone is starting from the same place. Equity, on the other hand, is about fairness, and ensuring people get access to the same opportunities. Sometimes our differences and/or history can create barriers to participation, so we must first ensure equity before we can enjoy equality.

3. Gender perspective is the consideration of gender-based differences between women and men as reflected in their social roles and interactions, and in the distribution of power and access to resources. This means taking these differences into account when making decisions or developing policies that impact women.

4. Conversely, being gender blind is the disregard for these differences as a significant factor in interactions between people. The problem with this is that gender blindness can downplay the existence of gender differences, which can reinforce existing gender inequality.

5. Quotas and targets can be used as temporary measures to 'even up the playing field'. Women and men can dismiss quotas as being exclusive of merit and perpetuate the notion of incompetent women being selected over competent men for promotion in a system that has overlooked qualified women for decades.

Five

Impact of sexual assault and harassment

Sexist jokes are often dismissed or excused as harmless fun. Yet they have real, negative effects in the world. They are linked to sexist and violent behaviour, they worsen gender inequalities, and they increase tolerance for violence against women.

Dr Michael Flood, Australian sociologist and Associate Professor, Queensland University of Technology

No doubt you've heard about the #MeToo movement—unless you've been living under a mushroom. #MeToo gained traction in 2017 in the US as a hashtag on social media, popularised by American actress Alyssa Milano, in an attempt to demonstrate the widespread prevalence of sexual assault and harassment, especially in the workplace. It followed several sexual abuse allegations against Harvey Weinstein, an American film producer. Milano encouraged victims of sexual harassment to tweet about it and 'give people a sense of the magnitude of the problem'.

For the record, the term 'Me Too', and the Me Too movement was founded by Tarana Burke, an American social activist and community organiser, in 2006. And I was privileged to meet Tarana in New York in late 2017, when I was seconded to UN Women Headquarters (HQ) as a policy specialist on sexual exploitation and abuse. Tarana is a softly spoken, kind and compassionate woman who has done so much to put the spotlight on the issue of sexual violence.

In a small conference room in the UN Women HQ, located in the Daily News building on 220 East 42nd St (you know, the one featured in 1978's *Superman: The Movie*), Tarana addressed a small group of UN Women staff.

She spoke movingly of her own experience with sexual violence as a child and a teenager. Her mother supported her recovery and encouraged her to be involved in working to improve the lives of young girls living in marginalised communities. She began to work with survivors of sexual violence and, in 2006, began using the phrase 'Me Too' to raise awareness of the pervasiveness of sexual abuse and assault in society.

And from this, the #MeToo movement was then projected into the limelight by Milano and has become a call to arms around the world as countries, organisations, communities and individuals grapple with this issue.

My own journey in the military began with a sexual assault (I did say this story would be warts and all). I was twenty years old and in my second year of training. I was posted to a Navy base for a course and I lived in a room in an officer's mess on the base. A place where I thought I was safe and protected.

And one night a terrible thing happened. We had a formal dinner, on duty, in uniform, and I drank too much. I remember distinctly two classmates getting me safely to my room and on the bed.

Later that night I was raped by a sailor, in my own room. I had no control. I was violated in a way I had never imagined.

This was not supposed to happen.

Can you imagine the impact of something like this?

I didn't report it at the time. The Navy then didn't have the mechanisms to respond to such complaints. I doubt I would have been believed—the early 1980s was a time when women were still in their respective female services, sexual harassment in the workplace was rife, pornographic pictures adorned office walls and lockers, and sexual and demeaning jokes about women were common. I would have been accused of somehow leading him on.

So I got up the next morning and went to class and acted as though nothing had happened. Even though I had to see him every day as he worked in the officer's mess.

I'm not telling you the story for sympathy; I'm a survivor, not a victim.

I raised the flag of victory because this experience gave me my purpose and my passion; it made me who I am today. And my experience did for me what Tarana's experience did for her. It gave her a purpose and a passion, and she has never wavered, publicly or privately, from her path. I feel it was the same for me.

My own experience with this, and many other instances of sexual harassment during the 1980s and 1990s, held me in good stead for later roles. I'm sure you can imagine how passionate I was about preventing this insidious behaviour and supporting women if they had experienced it. Even as late as 2010, 23 per cent of all complaints of unacceptable behaviour in the Navy workplace related to sexual harassment and sexual assault. When Navy introduced a Good Working Relationships program in the mid-1990s, I trained as an equity adviser, someone who could advise victims about their options for resolution.

Later, as the (inaugural) Navy Women's Strategic Adviser (the first of many inaugural gender roles for me as you will read about later in the book), I led a small team in developing a Navy-wide preventative program aimed at genuinely engaging all Navy people in discussions about the impact of unacceptable behaviour, including sexual harassment and sexual assault, in the workplace. 'Navigating the Change: Understanding the Impact of Unacceptable Behaviour' was launched by Rear Admiral Trevor Jones, then Deputy Chief of Navy, in August 2010. All Navy personnel completed this training by 2011. This program was one of many complementary measures, created as part of Navy's cultural reform program (New Generation Navy (NGN)) and designed to reinforce positive, respectful behaviours in the workplace that encouraged productivity, efficiency and good teamwork.

With this, I felt confident we were taking steps in the right direction.

Sexual assault and harassment today

You might say, okay, my experience was quite some time ago. Yes, it was. But clearly, as the Me Too movement shows, sexual assault and harassment is still a problem in workplaces today and a significant problem for many women in male-dominated professions even as I write.

Elizabeth Broderick's review into the treatment of women in the ADF in 2012 highlighted this. Interestingly, her report identified that women were much more likely to experience sexual harassment in the ADF than men. In the five years prior to 2012, 25.9 per cent of women and 10.5 per cent of men in the ADF had experienced sexual harassment in an ADF workplace. This compared to prevalence rates in a National Survey (by Roy Morgan Research) of 25.3 per cent of women and 16.2 per cent of men in the same time period.

Well, they do say the military is a microcosm of society, so perhaps this is to be expected.

In the ADF's case, the Broderick Review found that strong policies and mechanisms were now in place to address complaints of this nature; however, while the military's senior leadership had taken steps to actively create a culture where sexual misconduct and abuse was not tolerated, effective or appropriate tools were not available to enhance healthy and respectful sexual attitudes and behaviours. But the problem is greater than just armed forces. In chapter 1, I mention Elizabeth Broderick's 2019 review into the NSW Police Force, which also found a high level of sexual harassment. A survey conducted as part of the review revealed that one in three policewomen (34 per cent) had experienced sexual harassment in the course of their duties or at a work-related event, from a colleague, in the past five years.

Similarly, a culture of male dominance in Australian rural work-places is a key explainer for the high rate of sexual harassment for rural women. Researchers Skype Saunders and Patricia Easteal interviewed 84 female employees from regional and remote areas of Western Australia, the Northern Territory, South Australia and New South Wales.

They found that 73 per cent of rural women had experienced sexual harassment at work. This is compared to 25 per cent of women

Australia-wide. The research showed that women in these workplaces experienced similar issues to those in unrelated male-dominated professions.

And the statistics keep coming. In 2019, a survey of female lawyers in NSW, Australia, by the Women Lawyers Association of NSW, found more than 70 per cent of respondents reported sexual harassment occurring in the workplace or at social events. In the law profession, women make up 49 per cent of practising solicitors, but only 23 per cent of barristers, and fewer than 25 per cent of law firm partners in Australia.

The survey found that 'in an environment where junior roles are dominated by women and the most senior roles are dominated by men, there are unequal power relations between men and women'. Of the 70 per cent who reported sexual harassment, almost 50 per cent said the harasser was their manager and, in three cases, they were allegedly harassed by a judge.

Statistics from the AHRC 2018 report on sexual harassment in the workplace found the following: Women were clearly more likely than men to have been sexually harassed in the mining industry, with an estimated 74 per cent of women in this industry having experienced workplace sexual harassment in the past five years, compared with 32 per cent of men. Similarly, in construction, an estimated 51 per cent of women experienced workplace sexual harassment compared with 12 per cent of men.

And, of course, this isn't just happening in Australia—other countries are experiencing this as well. As recently as 2018, Chicago Women in Trades, a community-based organisation in the US committed to providing quality training and resources for women seeking to build successful careers, were forced to release a #MeToo paper on preventing and addressing sexual harassment in the trades industry.

Citing statistics like women comprising less than 1 to 3 per cent of workers in occupations such as electrician, machinist, transit vehicle mechanic or welder, their paper was aimed at industry and public policy-makers, and outlined the impact of sexual harassment on women and their organisations and offered training and public policy development support.

But, tellingly, the paper highlighted several indicators for high levels of sexual harassment of women in male-dominated professions. These indicators include:

- women being in the minority
- a macho culture and existing gendered stereotypes
- complaints being met with retaliation.

Nike is yet another example. (Yes, they just keep coming.) In 2018, a revolt led by women at Nike in Beaverton, Oregon, US, resulted in a number of male executives leaving the company. The revolt stemmed from a climate of toxic masculinity, where women were routinely subjected to sexual harassment, sexual abuse, exclusion, bullying and intimidation. Covertly, a group of women surveyed their female peers, and the results were handed directly to Nike's CEO, Marc Parker. Their findings set off an upheaval in the executive ranks. Nike's inspirational slogan, Just Do it, came to mean something else. This was Nike's #MeToo moment.

None of these things is new.

#MeToo was, and continues to be, all about calling out the abuse, by men, of the power, influence and control they hold within their industries. The fact that sexual harassment or abuse continues in male-dominated professions today is reflective of society's attitudes towards women and gender equality.

Even as I write, and despite the already mentioned statistics relating to professional women, a young military colleague shared with me a comment by a senior officer that quite frankly blew me away. He said, 'If women stopped acting like tarts, they'd stop being raped'. This, coming from a supposedly educated and highly qualified leader of people, is victim-blaming at its best. Comments such as these put the onus back on women to take steps to avoid being harassed or raped.

A 2012 AHRC paper on bystander approaches to sexual harassment in the workplace (by Dr Michael Flood and Paula McDonald) found that sexual harassment was more prevalent in male-dominated occupations and work contexts than in gender balanced or female-dominated workplaces.

It also found that it was not the organisational sex-ratio of the workplace per se that was associated with an increased likelihood of sexual harassment. Rather, the likelihood increased in organisational environments that were hierarchical, especially blue-collar, male-dominated settings where cultural norms were associated with bravado and posturing and where the denigration of feminine behaviours was sanctioned.

Finally, the research demonstrated that sexual harassment is more pervasive in organisations that show low sensitivity to the problem of balancing work and personal obligations and where the culture is job- or performance-oriented rather than employee-oriented.

LINKS BETWEEN SEXIST BEHAVIOUR AND SEXUAL HARASSMENT AND ASSAULT

Separately to the research discussed in the preceding section, Dr Flood wrote an article in June 2019 about the link between sexist behaviour and a willingness to use violence against women which, in turn, worsens existing gender inequalities. I cite Dr Flood as a credible researcher and academic on violence against women, fathering, pro-feminism, domestic violence, the effects of pornography on young people, safe sex among heterosexual men, men's movements as a backlash to the feminist movement, men's relationships with each other and with women, homophobia, men's health, and gender justice.

In his 2019 article, Dr Flood explained that:

- sexist jokes have an impact on women by making them feel unwelcome in the workplace and activating 'stereotype threat' in which women are or feel themselves to be at risk of conforming to stereotypes about their social group

- sexist jokes can impact men's prejudices against women

- exposure to sexist and violence-supportive jokes increases men's tolerance and support for violence against women.

Dr Flood also discussed the 'pyramid' effect of these types of behaviour and attitudes, where this kind of increased tolerance and support for sexist jokes, prejudice and violence against women is ultimately linked to more serious crimes by men against women, including rape, sexual assault, physical, emotional and financial abuse, and murder.

The reason I'm highlighting this is to demonstrate research that indicates the prevailing behaviours and attitudes of many (but #notallmen) men (in 2019!) have an impact on the level of equality enjoyed by men and women in their organisations and workplaces.

One of the more interesting but less common aspects of sexual harassment in male-dominated occupations is the underlying premise that society still sees some jobs as male — that is, not just men's work but also a core definition of masculinity.

An article in the *New York Times*, in early 2018[1], suggested that this dynamic played out in workplaces of all classes, but was particularly prevalent in blue-collar work (think construction sites, mines or even shipyards) that once embodied 'a kind of manly trifecta: they paid a breadwinner's wage, embodied strength and formed the backbone of the American economy'.

The upshot of this dynamic is that women become so scarce in these workplaces that, when they do enter them, the men refuse to see them as women. They call them obscene names and suggest the women must have a penis or be lesbians. They don't see the women as equals.

The article cited the research of Professor Abigail Saguy, who found lesbians were seen as less threatening in these scenarios, not fully women. She also found that women who went along with the banter were seen as either coming on to men or less competent in a workplace culture where proficiency is defined in masculine terms. She said, 'Sexual harassment is often a way in which the men reaffirm women's femininity, say this is who you are, back in your place.' Finally, she argued that as women were moving into these masculine occupations, and could do the job, this threatened men's masculinity.

Now, I'm not suggesting this is the case for all my male colleagues and, I'm sure, here in Australia, we like to think we're doing much better than most.

---

1   https://www.nytimes.com/2018/02/08/sunday-review/sexual-harassment-masculine-jobs.html.

But from what I have seen and experienced over my service career, women often have, or felt the need to, become, 'one of the boys' in order to be accepted.

They have adopted the masculinity of the culture, and maybe this has protected them from sexual harassment because they've been too afraid to show their femininity in a role previously done by men.

I could go on with many more examples, but suffice to say, can you still believe that gender equality exists in your organisation, when sexual harassment and, in some cases, sexual abuse prevails?

How can we believe in gender equality when women cannot be their true, authentic selves, for fear of being ostracised or harassed?

MY TOP 5 TIPS

1. Several indicators exist for high levels of sexual harassment of women in male-dominated professions: where women are in the minority, where a macho culture exists, where there are gendered stereotypes, and where retaliation occurs for complaining.

2. The fact that sexual harassment or abuse continues in male-dominated professions today is reflective of society's attitudes towards women and gender equality.

3. One of the more interesting but less common aspects of sexual harassment in male-dominated occupations is the underlying premise that society still sees some jobs as male — not just men's work but also a core definition of masculinity.

4. Women often have, or felt the need to, become, 'one of the boys' in order to be accepted. They have adopted the masculinity of the culture, maybe to protect themselves from sexual harassment, and maybe because they've been too afraid to show their femininity in a role previously done by men.

5. The prevalence of sexual harassment and abuse in workplaces undermines gender equality, and disables women from being their true, authentic selves.

Six

What does all this mean?

You must do the thing you think you cannot do.

Eleanor Roosevelt

Well, let me be clear. Despite what you might think is a lot of negativity around working in male-dominated occupations in the preceding chapters, I'm merely setting the context in which women work.

Not all women have experienced sexual harassment or sexual abuse. Not all women feel disadvantaged by being a woman in a traditionally male occupation. Not all women have experienced unconscious bias, disrespect, or 'toxic' masculinity in the workplace.

Many women feel they have been promoted, selected for opportunities or advanced in their careers on a firm belief in merit. Not all women believe they are not treated equally. #Notallwomen

But it is clear from the evidence, research and anecdotes that women do suffer from these things.

It is also clear that many of these male-dominated organisations, like the armed forces and police, are welcoming not only independent reviews into their culture, systems and processes, but also the change and transformation that comes with them.

Many are led by senior (in the main, male) leaders who have the vision to see that their organisations will be better equipped for contemporary issues if they have a gender diverse and inclusive workforce.

So, the purpose of my book is not to help organisations do this. People such as already mentioned Elizabeth Broderick, a highly regarded lawyer, previous Australian Sex Discrimination commissioner and gender expert, and organisations such as the AHRC have the authority and credibility to deliver strategies to achieve equality and diversity.

What I want to help build through this book is the power within yourself to meet and overcome the challenges, obstacles, and barriers I've outlined in the chapters in this part, and to achieve your full potential in the occupation of your choice.

YOU CAN DO ANYTHING YOU THINK YOU CAN DO

Have you ever read the children's story *The Little Engine That Could*? The story, published in 1930, is used to teach children the value of optimism and hard work. Okay, it's an American children's fairy tale that can be read in about five minutes. But the lesson of a small train tugging a larger train over a mountain can help set you up for a lifetime of success.

In the story, the little blue engine agrees to pull a larger train over a mountain, a seemingly impossible task. The engine succeeds in pulling the train over the mountain while repeating its motto, 'I think I can'. As it nears the top of the grade, the little train slows down. However, it still keeps saying, 'I—think—I—can, I—think—I—can' until it reaches the top. Once going down the other side, the train congratulates itself by saying, 'I thought I could, I thought I could'.

What's the lesson, you ask? Quite simply, *you can do anything you think you can do.*

One of the constant themes emerging from my coaching of women is their limited belief in themselves—and in their ability to change their circumstances, their position, their relationships, their life—and their uncertainty about whether they have it within themselves to do this. Many don't think they can do something differently.

I hear a lot of, 'I can't do this', 'Why is this happening to me?' and 'What can you do to help me?'

Well, of course, the answer to the last question is, 'I can help you see that you can do this'.

From my experience, the answer lies in a positive mindset and telling yourself you can do it every day. As Tony Robbins, a world-renowned coaching guru, said,

> *The power of positive thinking is the ability to generate a feeling of certainty in yourself when nothing in the environment supports you.*

Positive thinking is a mental and emotional attitude that focuses on the bright side of life and expects positive results. A woman with positive thinking mentality anticipates happiness, health and success, and believes that she can overcome any obstacle and difficulty.

The power of positive thinking allows the woman to hear the voice of dissent and uncertainty, of not being good enough or even not 'knowing her place', but to then say to that voice, 'Thanks for that. I hear and acknowledge you, but I don't believe you'. Then she says, 'I know I can do this'.

I had to adopt this approach very early on in my career in the Australian military—a career spent overcoming systemic barriers, discrimination and inequality. A career spent surviving (but ultimately thriving) in an environment and culture of sexist and abusive behaviour and attitudes by men towards women. I had to build resilience with every knock along the way and learn something from the experience, whether positive or negative. I had to find the silver lining without being too 'Pollyanna-ish' about it. I said to myself, 'I've got this, I can do it'.

What I want to see is you adopting the five strategies in the next part of this book that I believe will give you the strength, self-belief, self-confidence, passion and purposeful leadership to enable you to 'be what you can't see' and thrive in your profession.

This is your right.

#Allwomen It's time to grab your ruler, sextant and chart, and begin to sail against the wind and plot a new course for your life!

My top 5 tips

1. Like the Little Engine That Could, you can do anything you think you can do.

2. Your limited belief in yourself can be overcome.

3. The power of positive thinking is the ability to generate a feeling of certainty in yourself when nothing in the environment supports you.

4. With positive thinking you can anticipate happiness, health and success, and believe that you can overcome any obstacle and difficulty.

5. Find the silver lining in every negative experience, and tell yourself you've got this.

Part Two

CHARTING A NEW COURSE

I'm not afraid of storms,
for I'm learning to sail my ship.

Louisa May Alcott

Seven

Be what you
can't see

*Show me how to take who I am, who I want to be, and
what I can do, and use it for a purpose greater than myself.*

Martin Luther King Jr

Okay, I know I always start chapters with a quote from someone else,
but here I also want to quote myself. In an article about my life in
the Navy published in the *Sydney Morning Herald* and its subsidiary
newspapers around Australia in late 2018, my final words quoted were
the following:

> People often say to young people, 'You can't be what you can't see',
> and we argue that we need to have role models, for young girls to see
> that there are women pilots, engineers, and all these other opportunities
> that exist ... On the other hand, I would also say you can be what
> you can't see, because as the world evolves, and as workplaces evolve,
> there's always going to be firsts.

I've spent a good six chapters on setting the current scene, in Australia
and across the world, because I think it's important to understand
the context, historically and contemporaneously, in which women
operate in male-dominated professions. If you've read the preceding
chapters, where are your thoughts now about gender equality, the use
of quotas, or the 'merit' myth?

Perhaps your thoughts are unchanged. Perhaps you already knew these issues have been around a long time and sadly remain, and we women must navigate them as best we can in a way that allows us to be as authentic as possible, that enables us to reach our full potential, and aspire to have fulfilling and satisfying careers. Perhaps you jumped straight to this chapter to find out how!

For me, carving out a career and aspiring to what I have now came from one single incident that occurred early in my career (which I talk about in chapter 5). As I outline, this was a defining moment, where I was given clarity around my purpose and my passion. I didn't know where I was headed, however, so I was literally navigating unchartered waters.

That career was a life of many 'firsts' for women, and I've already mentioned some of those firsts in the chapters in part 1: first military woman to trek Kokoda in PNG in 1986, and the first of two senior female logistics officers to serve at sea in 1996 are just two examples.

So, I've known throughout my career that, regardless of where my career would take me, I had to step up, take action, and be that first, be that thing I couldn't see. This meant knowing who I was, what I needed to do, and what results or outcomes I was looking for.

BE-DO-HAVE COACHING MODEL

Perhaps you've already come across the BE-DO-HAVE coaching model, based on the principle that you have to first BE the person that you ultimately want to be, then DO the actions this person would do and finally you will HAVE the things that that person would have.

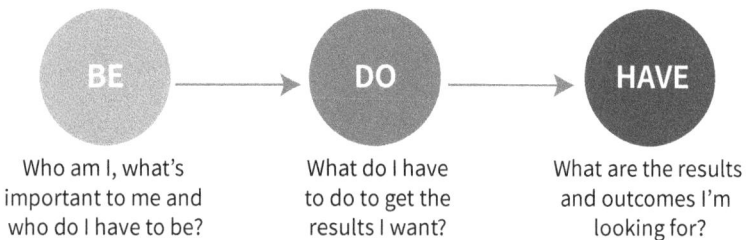

BE	DO	HAVE
Who am I, what's important to me and who do I have to be?	What do I have to do to get the results I want?	What are the results and outcomes I'm looking for?

The philosophy of BE-DO-HAVE, which some say was first introduced by L. Ron Hubbard in his book *Conditions of Existence*, refers to the attitude and mind shift that has to occur in order for all of us to enjoy the kind of life we want.

Larger-than-life personalities such as Anthony Robbins and Stephen Covey use this model, particularly in their writing.

The simple three-step process helps you achieve your vision and goals. You just need to ask yourself:

1. *Who am I being and who do I have to BE?* You can take 'being' as your nature or essence, which is the foundation for your qualities, roles and behaviours.

   In my case, I had the clarity of who I wanted to BE: a woman who supported and empowered other women so that they could be spared from my lived experiences. This was purpose and vision. I wanted to BE that woman who would survive countless 'firsts' as barriers were broken and discrimination and inequality were overcome and use that experience to give back to my tribe. I knew I had to BE what I couldn't see.

2. *What do I have to DO to get the results or outcomes I want?* Once the new way of BEing has been created, possible courses of action begin to emerge, and you are called into action and propelled into the future and to manifesting our goals.

   For me, this meant saying yes to opportunities because they supported my purpose. This meant:

   - serving at sea as a senior maritime logistics officer and only one of two women in a crew of 212, and trekking Kokoda in PNG with an all-male team
   - building a childcare centre in a Navy base of mostly male apprentices and staff (if you want to know more about building a childcare centre in a military base, see chapter 12)
   - embarking on a second career promoting women's rights to participation and representation in armed forces against a fixed organisational mindset that judged equality for woman on the basis they could meet the male benchmarks.

   The DO-ing became about finding my strengths, understanding my beliefs and values, and taking action. It meant building resilience with every knock along the way and learning something from the experience, whether positive or negative. It meant finding the silver lining. And this enabled me to develop and grow as that person I wanted to BE.

The major DO-ing was in fact taking the long-term view of my career, thinking B.I.G. (brave and important goals), and setting out to achieve them. The DO-ing was setting my sights on meeting specific career milestones, and having a vision of how my purpose and passion could affect the organisation and the women in it.

3. *What are the results or outcomes that I'm looking for (the 'HAVE')?* Thinking B.I.G. and having my vision gave me the HAVE.

I spent the last ten years in the military contributing to significant cultural change around behaviour and attitudes towards others. At home in Australia, I led the implementation of international conventions and commitments on women's roles in peace and security efforts. Overseas, I promoted the Australian military's progress on the participation and representation of women. Nationally and internationally, I represented Australia, in numerous forums, on gender and women in the armed forces.

With all the insights gained from my DO-ing, BE-ing and HAVE-ing, I then developed my Be What You Can't See model.

BE WHAT YOU CAN'T SEE MODEL

As I highlighted at the start of this chapter, the idea that 'you can be what you can't see' is one I coined in a 2018 newspaper article. When quoted in this article, I was talking about the lack of role models in many non-traditional industries, and the need for women to step up and take on that role.

I've already discussed the view that 'you can't be it if you can't see it', and that this is true to a certain extent. I know you may feel you need to see role models before you can see something is possible. But I also believe that you can be what you *can't* see if you are brave enough and focused enough, and are willing to make the foray into non-traditional roles.

And, of course, we wouldn't even be having this conversation without the women who so bravely fought for feminism, equal rights and human rights over the past century or so. They were also visionaries, ambitious, courageous, and emotionally strong women who fought relentlessly so we could enjoy the fruits of their labour.

Well, here we are, in 2019, still needing to be visionary, courageous and emotionally strong in the face of the challenges that continue to exist in our workplaces. We are fighting not just for systemic equality in the workplace—including equality in the systems, policies and mechanisms—but also true equality in how men and women treat and value each other.

So, I took all I've learnt about how to be all these things—visionary, courageous and emotionally strong—and built the Be What You Can't See model, shown in full in the following figure.

As you can see, the model starts with YOU and is then broken into five strategies, each with a WHAT, YOU and CAN'T SEE element—that is, who you need to BE, to do WHAT you need to do, to get the results or outcomes YOU want but CAN'T SEE. Over the coming chapters, I explain each of the five strategies in detail.

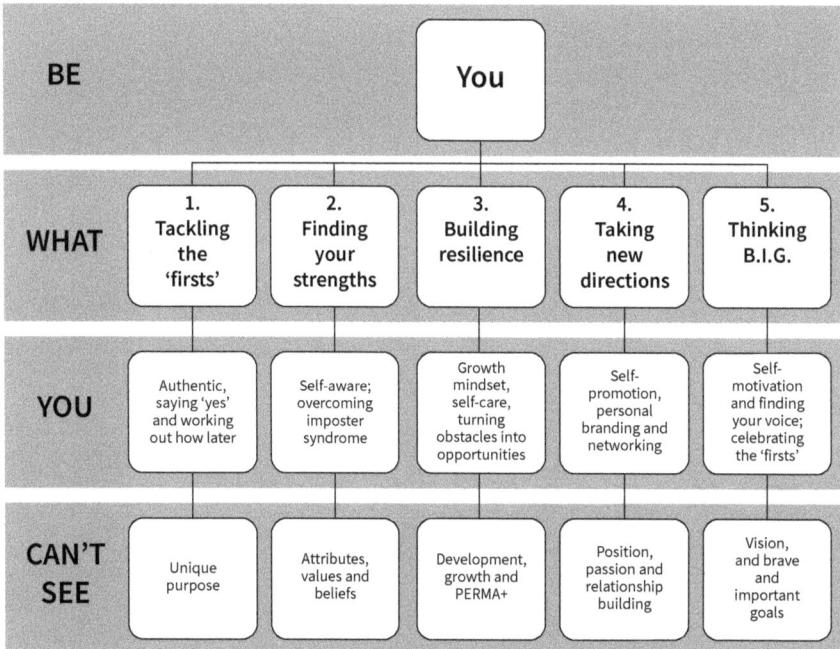

BE	You				
WHAT	1. Tackling the 'firsts'	2. Finding your strengths	3. Building resilience	4. Taking new directions	5. Thinking B.I.G.
YOU	Authentic, saying 'yes' and working out how later	Self-aware; overcoming imposter syndrome	Growth mindset, self-care, turning obstacles into opportunities	Self-promotion, personal branding and networking	Self-motivation and finding your voice; celebrating the 'firsts'
CAN'T SEE	Unique purpose	Attributes, values and beliefs	Development, growth and PERMA+	Position, passion and relationship building	Vision, and brave and important goals

MY TOP 5 TIPS

1. We women must navigate all the issues that arise in male-dominated workplaces as best we can in a way that allows us to be as authentic as possible, that enables us to reach our full potential, and aspire to have fulfilling and satisfying careers.

2. The BE-DO-HAVE coaching model is based on the principle that you have to first BE the person that you ultimately want to be, then DO the actions this person would do and finally you will HAVE the things that that person would have.

3. A common view that 'you can't be it if you can't see it', and this is true to a certain extent. I know you may feel you need to see role models before you can see something is possible. But I also believe that you can also 'be what you can't see' if you are brave enough and focused enough, and willing to make the foray into non-traditional roles.

4. In 2019, we women still need to be visionary, courageous and emotionally strong in the face of the challenges that continue to exist in our workplaces.

5. The Be What You Can't See model outlines who you need to BE, to do WHAT you need to do, to get the results or outcomes YOU want but CAN'T SEE. Follow me on this journey!

Eight

Tackling the firsts

She had the courage to pattern her life
after a woman — herself.

Michael Thomas Kelly, poet

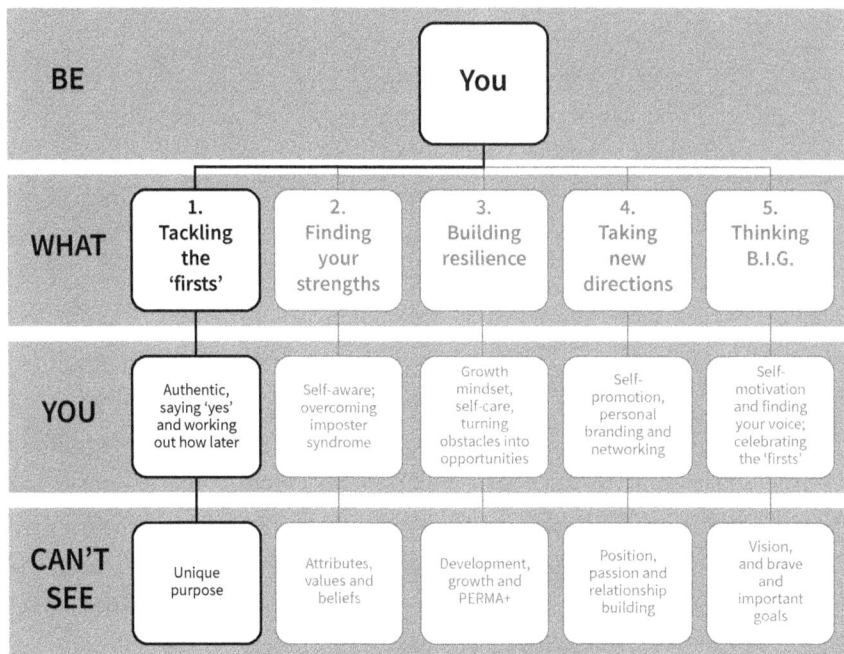

		1.	2.	3.	4.	5.
BE				You		
WHAT		1. Tackling the 'firsts'	2. Finding your strengths	3. Building resilience	4. Taking new directions	5. Thinking B.I.G.
YOU		Authentic, saying 'yes' and working out how later	Self-aware; overcoming imposter syndrome	Growth mindset, self-care, turning obstacles into opportunities	Self-promotion, personal branding and networking	Self-motivation and finding your voice; celebrating the 'firsts'
CAN'T SEE		Unique purpose	Attributes, values and beliefs	Development, growth and PERMA+	Position, passion and relationship building	Vision, and brave and important goals

THE WHAT: STEP UP AND TACKLE THE FIRSTS

When I joined the Navy (the WRANS) in 1981 I thought it was a thoroughly modern Navy and I was a thoroughly modern Millie! I'd been brought up to believe I could do whatever I wanted in life.

At that time, women only comprised about 7 per cent of the Navy workforce.

As I've already mentioned, I joined as a logistics officer which had only opened to women a couple of years prior. And I've also talked about how I was first accused of only joining the Navy to find a husband and then later criticised for not wearing makeup or tying my shoelaces the right way. (And I remember thinking, *Wow! Is this what is really important? How about how I do my job or my potential for promotion?* I didn't even know there was a specific way to tie laces!)

By this stage, I was beginning to feel like I was in a 1950s movie and couldn't get out of it! It wasn't really a great start, but I had made a commitment, initially a nine-year contract, and I was determined to see it through.

But three major game changers occurred during my career that affected women and enabled them to become those 'firsts'.

I've already mentioned these changes as well, but let me provide a little more detail on these changes, and their effects, here:

1. *The introduction of the Sex Discrimination Act in 1984:* This required the WRANS to disband and women were integrated into the RAN, the 'men's service.' For the first time, men and women were competing for promotions, training opportunities, and postings — of course, only within those occupations in which women were allowed.

2. *The government's lift in the early 1990s of the gender restrictions on combat-related roles:* This enabled greater numbers of women to take up roles previously denied to them, including becoming pilots, warfare officers and engineers, and opening positions on ships.

3. *The government's lift in 2011 of all gender restrictions:* Women could now be employed in combat roles such as infantry, artillery, air defence guards and our equivalent of Navy SEALs.

Passing Out Parade, Royal Australian Naval College, Jervis Bay, 1981 (me on far right)

Me aged 20 years at HMAS *Cerberus*, 1982

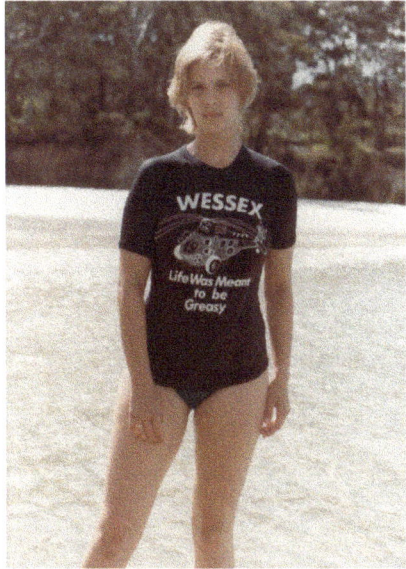

Celebrating 723SQN's Wessex Helicopter birthday, around 1984

Filming of a recruiting advertisement,
Royal Australian Naval College, 1984

Opening of Little Pelican's Child Care
Centre, HMAS *Nirimba*, NSW, with
the Commanding Officer, Captain
Brian Swan, RAN, and then Minister
for Defence, Science and Personnel,
Gordon Bilney, 1992

Last day of Kokoda Trek, me in front, Lieutenant Graham Pedley, RAN, on right
back with his 'skirt', Papua New Guinea, 1986

My Navy class (me at front far right), RANC, Jervis Bay, 1981

Leading an all-male formation on parade, HMAS *Nirimba*, NSW, around 1989-90

Receiving the Lonsdale Medallion
from then Chief of Navy, VADM
Rod Taylor, AO, RAN, Navy Staff
College, HMAS *Penguin*, NSW, 1993

Helicopter Control Officer duties on
HMAS *Swan*, 1996

With colleagues at Diego Garcia, 2002

Finalist in 2011 Telstra Business Women's Awards, with then Chief of Defence
Force (now Governor General) General David Hurley, AC, DSC, FTSE, then
Chief of Navy, Vice Admiral Ray Griggs, AO, CSC, RAN and then Chief of Air
Force, AVM Mark Binskin, AC, along with fellow finalist, Rear Admiral Robyn
Walker, RAN

With the then Governor General, Dame Quentin Bryce, AD, CVO, and two
of my mentees, then Leading Seaman (now Lieutenant) Kristy Bates, and then
Leading Seaman (now Mrs) Trish Dollisson at an International Women's Day
event, 2012

With international colleagues at the NATO Committee on Gender Perspective at NATO Headquarters, Brussels, 2012

With now Lieutenant General Jody Osterman, USMC, in Kabul, 2013

With fellow military and civilian gender advisers in Kabul, 2013

With international colleagues and local girls, International Women's Day, Kabul, 2013

Meeting policewomen at Kabul City Police Station, 2013

Presentation of my NATO medal, Kabul, 2013

For International Women's Day event in Middle East, Kabul, 2013

Promoted to temporary Captain, 2013

Me with the then Governor General, Dame Quentin Bryce, AD, CVO on the occasion of my investiture of a Conspicuous Service Medal, Government House, Canberra, 2013

At the investiture of my Conspicuous Service Medal, Government House Canberra, 2013, with mum, Taylah and Chaeleigh

With Elizabeth Broderick, then Sex Discrimination Commissioner, at NATO Headquarters, Brussels, for launch for NATO project 'UNSCR 1325 Reload', 2015

Outside the old NATO Headquarters, Brussels, 2015

With national and international colleagues in Government House, NSW, with then Governor David Hurley, AC, DSC, FTSE, 2015

Preparing for Anzac Day 2015

Meetings with security sector personnel and UN Women, Ukraine, 2017

With Tarana Burke, founder of #MeToo,
UN Women Headquarters, New York, 2017

With Executive Director UN Women Phumzile Mlambo-Ngcuka, and Chief of
Peace and Security, Paivi Kannisto, UN Women Headquarters, New York, 2017

The main street of Rye, New York, where I lived, 2017–18

Marching with the Naval Women's Association on Anzac Day, 2018, along with Army colleague Narelle Powers

On my Honda VTR 250

With my daughters Taylah and Chaeleigh

Textile artwork by Lucy Sattler

Winning Most Inspirational Y at the YFactor Awards, Gold Coast, 2019

My father, Flying Officer Graham Scutt, RAAF

My mother, Aircraftswomen Jeanette Dunn, RAAF

So, as you can imagine, from 1984 the time was ripe for women to step up and take on challenges that had previously been denied to them, and to be those first women to do something new. I certainly took advantage of every opportunity, going into the unknown, saying yes and working out how later, because I had a sense of purpose—to make my mark in this very male-dominated profession and show them that women were as equally important to the military's mission.

THE YOU: SAY YES AND WORK IT OUT LATER

Richard Branson, business magnate, investor, author and philanthropist, once said, 'If someone offers you an amazing opportunity and you are not sure you can do it, say yes and learn how to do it later.'

Knowing my purpose enabled me to say yes to a number of opportunities that ultimately fulfilled my purpose and my passion, and took my career in a completely different direction than I had anticipated. One thing led to another and that led to another.

Let me go back as far as 2002. I had returned from maternity leave with my second daughter in late 2000 into a finance role in the Navy HQ. The role wasn't so exciting but a normal part of my logistics occupation.

A complaint from military personnel about improper conduct by a few sailors on one of our warships visiting Diego Garcia (a tiny British-owned, US–run island in the Indian Ocean) in late 2001 prompted a request from the then Chief of Navy in early January 2002 that I join a small team heading there to investigate.

At the same time, similar complaints had been made about sailors' behaviour on Christmas Island, an Australian external territory located in the Indian Ocean. The media reports about the allegations were extensive and called into question the Navy's values and codes of conduct.

So, I returned from Diego Garcia to an invitation by the Chief of Navy to head up a directorate of Navy organisational culture. Well, it was just me in the 'team', but it was the beginning of the Navy starting to take sailors' poor behaviour more seriously because it was damaging the Navy's reputation as a professional fighting force.

I said yes because I thought I might have an opportunity to address the culture of sexual harassment and poor treatment of women by male sailors that existed at the time. I said yes even though I'd been given no job description and I had to create the role.

This meant the next two years were spent focusing on Navy's values, redefining Navy's mission and building a worthy and reputable brand. All of this was captured by the slogan 'Serving in Australia's Navy' and through providing clearly defined guidance on Chief of Navy's expectations of behaviour, professional reputation, and adhering to Navy's values. This early work subsequently led to Navy's landmark cultural reform program NGN, which commenced in 2009. At that time, I was (again) fortunate to be invited to head up the cultural pillar of that program. I think I was becoming known as 'that gender diversity chick'!

In 2004, I transferred to the Reserves for a period of five years so I could have more flexibility around my working hours with two small children. During this time I continued to support the Navy as an investigator for Navy member's complaints about administrative decisions affecting their service. This was a great period in my life where, as I had then recently become a single mum, I was able to continue my military service but at a more flexible pace so I could manage my young family.

But in 2008 (with both children in school), I was eager to return and, lo and behold, they wanted me back again in organisational culture. Well, to be honest, I think it was because no one else wanted to do it!

This time I focused strongly on developing programs for women to give them the skills and confidence to set and achieve their career goals. I was fortunate to work for an amazing Deputy Chief of Navy, Rear Admiral Davyd Thomas, RAN, who I credit with giving me the confidence, the space—and the funding—to drive reform around women's participation. During this time, I created and implemented Navy women's leadership, mentoring and networking programs, which continue to be funded and operated today. This was one of my greatest accomplishments, and the joy I gained from seeing women grow and advance as a result of it was immeasurable.

Davyd's retired now but I enjoy seeing him occasionally in my local café and spinning some yarns!

Then, as I mentioned previously, in 2009, the Navy initiated NGN. I'm not going to go into a heap of detail about this (you can Google it if you'd like to find out more about the initiatives involved and reasons behind them) but I will say that NGN has been so successful that its work continues even today. When NGN was launched, the then Chief of Navy, Vice Admiral Russ Crane, RAN, said, 'improving Navy's culture was my number one priority'. As part of the reforms I was asked, given my then role, to join the team that was developing the program and head the cultural pillar (one of three pillars; the others were leadership and structure).

Now let me be clear: at the time, I was not an expert in organisational culture or reform (apart from my two stints in 2002 and 2008). But Navy had faith in me because of what I had already achieved, so I said yes, again, to a new role, and having to work it out as we went along.

To cut a long story short, women's leadership and the treatment of women continued to dominate the culture space so, in 2010, it was decided that I would be appointed to an inaugural strategic women's adviser role for Navy senior leadership. Again, I had to create the role, a challenge I eagerly accepted. My responsibilities included creating initiatives to support women's leadership development and advancement, and to advise Navy's senior leadership on ways to improve their recruitment and retention. I felt this was a her-storical step taken by Navy, and one that demonstrated their commitment to this issue. This role remains, and some terrific women continue to further evolve and progress gender mainstreaming across Navy. And, along the way, I was recognised for my meritorious service to women in the Navy with the award of a Conspicuous Service Medal in the 2013 Queen's Birthday Honours List—both a highlight for me, and a telling moment in the Navy's gender journey!

Can you see the path developing? Saying yes to the opportunities even though they were niche and emerging areas?

Hell, yeah, the ride didn't stop there. That role led me to work with NATO in Brussels in 2012. As the Navy women's strategic adviser and, at that time, the only women's adviser to a Chief of Service, I was situated well to be invited to attend the annual conference of the NATO committee on gender perspective as the Australian representative. (This committee is responsible for assessing women's participation in NATO member countries armed forces and developing contemporary approaches to NATO's peace and security efforts that ensure the inclusion of women in all aspects of conflict.)

As fate would have it, here I met Colonel Ingrid Gjerde, who I mentioned in chapter 1, who spoke about the role of NATO gender advisers in their operations in Afghanistan and Kosovo. I returned to Canberra after the conference and briefed the Deputy Chief of Navy, at that time Rear Admiral Trevor Jones, RAN (now retired), another inspiring and trusted mentor I was lucky to have. In my discussions with him, I particularly highlighted the role of gender advisers.

Well, damn, then another opportunity came along! Only a month later, Trevor stopped me in the hallway and said, 'You remember we were talking about gender advisers a few weeks ago? Well, Australia has been offered the opportunity to fill the gender adviser role in Afghanistan. Navy has the first rotation, so sort out your family, pack your bags, you're going in January'.

Now it made sense that I go, because at that time I was the only one who had some experience and some qualification around the whole NATO/gender adviser area. Of course, I said yes, even though I didn't have the opportunity to do the NATO gender adviser training at the Nordic Centre for Gender in Military Operations in Sweden before I got there. *No biggie*, I thought. I know what it's about.

Actually, sorting out my home life was more difficult—I was a single mother of two young girls, aged 13 and 15 at the time. Not the best age to leave but I so desperately wanted this gig. And I went, in January 2013.

My role was to implement and embed the NATO policy on gender perspective across all operations in Afghanistan, including counterinsurgency, stabilisation and civil-military activities. This policy was designed to translate political direction and guidance for NATO-led operations on the effective implementation of the UN Security Council Resolutions on Women, Peace and Security. These resolutions, now nine in number, provide an overarching framework on the way women can be better engaged in peace and security efforts, how their opportunities for leadership and participation can be improved, and how women's experiences and perspectives in conflict can be considered in all peace-building activities.

What I found when I arrived was a complete absence, at the operational command, of any understanding of what the NATO policy was, how the operational plans were required to comply with the policy, and even what 'gender' meant. As you could appreciate, I met with resistance and pushback. 'We're too busy fighting the war to worry about gender' was a quote that a colleague, who went to Afghanistan as a gender adviser after me, heard from a senior (male) officer!

But I had great support from two wonderful men, General Gus McLachlan (Australian Army) and Major General Jody Osterman, USMC, who headed up the two major operational divisions of plans and operations. They embraced the NATO policy and UN resolutions, supported me and my role without question, and facilitated the introduction of a framework that would embed gender perspective as a planning and operational requirement. Gus would often remark later, when reflecting on his gender experience in Afghanistan, that he was 'Wittwer-trained'. And even today, Jody, as a three-star ranked General and head of special operations command in the US Marine Corp, often remarks on aspects of gender at home that he had not considered prior to meeting me in Afghanistan. This was definitely a great example of using influence and building connections (which I describe in more detail later in the book) to achieve the impossible!

When I left in July 2013, I wasn't ready to come home. I felt I had more to do, and that I could do more to make a difference for both NATO and for Afghan women. Yet waiting for me at home was another opportunity!

I came into a role that had been created for me, to work directly for the CDF, to implement the military's responsibilities under an Australian Government NAP on women, peace and security. This involved pretty much what I had been doing in Afghanistan but on a larger scale, and in a more national context.

The NAP had a six-year life span (from 2012 to 2018) and involved other government agencies such as the Australian Federal Police, the Department of Foreign Affairs and Trade, the Australian Civil Military Centre (ACMC), and the Attorney-General's Department. The NAP's purpose was to articulate Australia's commitment to implement the UN resolutions on women, peace and security, to establish a whole-of-government approach to implementation, to identify the strategies and actions each agency would take, and to highlight some of the important work Australia was already doing to respond to women's needs, recognise their roles and promote their equal participation in peace and security efforts.

How could I say no—even when I was a team of one, with no resources, and just told to get on with it? I was still the only ADF member with the right qualifications, skills and experience to do this.

Okay, this is the last story. Arising out of our work on that NAP, the ADF created a five-year secondment to UN Women HQ in New York, to work in their peace and security section as a policy specialist on peacekeeping and sexual exploitation and abuse. I wrote the duty statement for the secondment and, given my previous experience, believed I was best placed to take the first rotation. And I was! This role was in a civilian capacity, and I was called upon to provide a military perspective on the work that UN Women was doing on peace and security around the world. On any given day in the role, I could be conducting training on gender equality and conflict-related sexual violence in peace keeping to Army personnel in Jordan, providing presentations to Ukrainian Armed Forces personnel on gender mainstreaming, or speaking at conferences and on panels in Spain, Italy or New York on sexual exploitation and abuse.

Ultimately the role was an amazing gift, allowing me to work on much broader gender issues than just those facing the military. For example, I participated in the development of a curriculum for the international female police officers' preparatory course for UN peacekeeping, and also worked with the Police Division in the Department of Peacekeeping Operations in UN headquarters to address systemic barriers to women's participation in peacekeeping. I supported and contributed to the conduct of a gender impact assessment (to see how men and women were affected by policies and procedures) of the Ukrainian defence and security sector agencies, and the subsequent development of a gender equality strategy.

Now you could argue that I didn't really have a plan for my career and that I only rolled with the punches as they came along.

But there was a pattern—I was offered these opportunities because I was in the right place and the right time with the right skills, and I just kept saying yes, even when I didn't initially know how I was going to do it.

All of these opportunities aligned with my WHY, my purpose and passion, so I jumped into them without a life vest, having enough faith in myself, telling myself I couldn't and wouldn't fail, and just drawing upon all my strengths and values to get it done.

Over the course of these roles I met with much resistance from women and men in my profession over the gender diversity initiatives the ADF was keenly implementing. Conversely, I also met with many other people from other government organisations, non-government organisations, international armed forces, academics and civil society who fuelled my passion for women's roles in peace and security.

As I discuss later in this chapter, author Simon Sinek has written (and spoken) a great deal about the importance of finding your WHY—that is, the reason behind your passion for doing something. For now, let me say I truly believe once you know your WHY, you'll find it easier to know which jobs and which opportunities you should or shouldn't take in your careers. Even if the choices or opportunities are unpopular, if they fit your WHY, it's up to you what you make of it and get out of it.

AUTHENTICITY AND OVERCOMING THE FEAR OF FEMININITY

Who do you need to BE to be able to step up and tackle the firsts, say yes and work it out later? You just need to be you, just your authentic self—someone not afraid to be themselves, and not afraid of their femininity.

Because let's face it, ladies, we are women. Putting on a uniform that looks like the blokes' doesn't make us less of a woman. Even though I was never one for make-up (as I've mentioned) until my later years, and even though we finally got trousers in the 1990s, I still fancied wearing a skirt and court shoes in the office from time to time. As did many of my female colleagues. Many still do.

So, what's there to be afraid of?

I recently read a lovely story of a young American woman, Mary, who had served in the US Air Force and later transitioned to corporate life, and then became a police officer. She says she refused to wear make-up in the military because she wanted to assimilate, to not appear feminine. She felt she had to maintain an androgynous appearance to be considered professional.

What she found in the corporate world were smart, organised, progressive and motivated women, who were also groomed, polished and beautiful. She subsequently underwent a makeover with make-up. But she said what was more important than that was her attitude adjustment about her personal appearance in a professional setting. She felt caring for her appearance made her comfortable and confident.

She said,

> For me, the choice to wear make-up isn't a means to distinguish myself from the boys, or to be more attractive to men. It's rooted in the belief that if I care about my appearance enough to make the effort, I'm sending a message that I care about myself, I care about my job, and I care about others.

I love that! She had found her authentic self.

But what does being authentic really mean?

Most dictionaries feature variations around the theme of being of undisputed origin and not a copy; genuine.

This means that when we are born, we are a blank page. We have the capacity within ourselves to take that page and choose what to write on it. You can choose what kind of person you want to BE, and choose your values, your aspirations and the principles by which you 'want to live your life. These may not come to you early in life, but may evolve over time as you become more conscious of your WHY.

If you need to, you can set your compass and head in a new direction—now, if you need to. If you're reading this book and don't already know your WHY, chart your new course now.

Often writing your pages is not easy. We fear judgement from others, we worry about failure—or success—and we look to others to provide answers because we don't think we have them. We also try to fit in, conform to our workplaces (much like I discussed in chapter 1). When we play by rules passed down through the generations, however, we can lose a part of ourselves. We can stop being authentic to a true BE-ing.

But the truth is only you can write your page.

This means focusing on self. BE-ing authentic is the first step to self, and (as covered in the previous chapter) BE-ing you will enable you to DO and to ultimately HAVE. It's who you are BE-ing, your 'self', that will inspire others, allow others to connect with you willingly, as they trust your judgment and your decisions. Leadership 101!

If being authentic also means not being afraid of your femininity in your male-dominated workplace, then do that.

The good news is that you don't have to create fanfare around your authenticity, or even the fact you are going on a journey to find it. People will see what your values are by the way you act, speak, think, make decisions and show emotional intelligence. Being authentic means you are living your values.

If you want to be authentic, just focus on writing that new page.

CHALLENGE

I challenge you to begin to step out in a whole new way; say yes even when you are afraid.

I challenge you to be honest rather than avoiding difficult conversations or saying what you think others want to hear.

I challenge you to ask for what you want every time.

Most of all, I challenge you to be yourself in every thought, act or spoken word.

So, are you up for the challenge?

For the next two weeks keep a journal to record all the ways you are not being authentic or honest. Check for patterns and themes. You may want to talk to a coach or mentor to find out why you do certain things.

Then find an affirmation that resonates well with you. I like the following:

'I dare to be myself, whatever that looks like.'

Write it on a sticky note and place it somewhere you'll see it often — your bathroom mirror, for example, or computer or refrigerator. Read your affirmation aloud every day and focus your actions on being authentic.

WHAT YOU CAN'T SEE: KNOW YOUR WHY

Once you're living more authentically, you can really get into the nitty-gritty of knowing your WHY. As you've probably already gathered, my view is that to be able to step up into the unknown, you need to know your WHY, your purpose, your true north. If you know your WHY, the HOW to DO something will take care of itself. German philosopher Frederick Nietzsche once wrote, 'If we have our own 'why' of life we shall get along with almost any 'how'.'

Importantly, if you know your purpose, you also tend to live a more meaningful life than those who don't.

Knowing your why is an important first step in figuring out how to achieve the goals that excite you and create the life you want.

You tend to live each day to the fullest, because you know who you're BE-ing, where you're coming from, and what you want to HAVE.

How do you get to your WHY? If you don't know it already, you need to make it the ultimate, all-consuming question to ask yourself.

In chapter 5, I talk about the defining moment in my life that gave me clarity around my purpose — to serve and support women — and

I never faltered from that sense of direction. This was my North Star and it became the guide I needed to take me in the direction I had chosen.

I wake up each day knowing that everything I do, everything I think about, serves that purpose. Even my work now as a consultant, coach and mentor is centred on empowering women to take leadership roles. I live my passion 100 per cent every day and it drives everything I do.

Can you say the same about your life?

But I know finding your WHY isn't always easy. As a coach, women often ask me, 'How do I find my WHY? How can I discover my purpose? How can I create goals if I don't know my purpose?' The following five-step process provides some help.

Step 1: Get clear on who you are — or want to BE

Some questions to ponder include:

- What do you want in life?
- What did you love doing when you were younger?
- What legacy do you want to leave?
- What do others say about you?
- What and who inspires you and why?
- Where do you add the greatest value?
- What are your greatest strengths? (More on this in the following chapter.)
- What keeps you awake at night?
- What are you good at?
- What makes you feel alive and energised?
- What do you believe in?
- What is your personal vision? (More on this in chapter 12.)
- What do you love doing the most?
- What and who motivates you?

- What are your standards and benchmarks in life?

- What won't you compromise on?

- What makes you unique?

- When have you been the happiest in life and why?

- What are you most proud of?

- What 'shoulds' are getting in the way of 'wants'?

- If money were no object, what would you be doing right now?

Step 2: List your interests and passions

These are the things that you enjoy spending time doing, either at work, at home, or in your community. They may be things that cause you to lose track of time when doing them!

Step 3: Write down what you love

Acknowledging the things and people you love can bring you closer to finding your purpose.

Step 4: Find your joy.

What makes you get up out of bed in the morning, or makes you late to bed at night? Think of all the things that spark joy in your life.

Step 5: Create your WHY statement

Finally, take all your insights from the preceding four steps and distil them into one or two sentences or a statement that you can live by. This statement should encapsulate why you are here, who you will BE, and how you DO what you need to do.

As mentioned, Simon Sinek is one thought leader who knows a lot about the importance of finding your WHY. In his book *Start with Why*, he created a 'Why Statement' template: *To … so that …*

The TO represents your contribution—the contribution you make to the lives of others through your WHY. And the SO THAT represents the impact of your contribution.

Here is Simon Sinek's WHY: '*To* inspire people to do the things that inspire them *so that*, together, we can change our world.'

And here is mine: *To* empower women *so that* they may create meaningful lives and reach their full potential.

What is your WHY? Take some time now to think more about it, and write down your statement in your journal. Frame it in Sinek's template: *To … so that …*

Knowing your WHY has many benefits, including:

- keeping you focused on the end game, so you can stay the course

- helping you set and achieve goals

- reminding you daily of your passions

- giving you clarity about all aspects of your life

- helping you make a greater impact with your actions

- enabling you to remain true to your core values (which I talk about in the next chapter)

- helping you become more flexible about change and challenges in life

- enabling you to find life, work and family more pleasurable and joyful.

So, I wake up each day eager to get on with my work, my writing and my projects because it is joyful.

And then, knowing my WHY makes it easier to say YES even if I don't know HOW to do it!

MY TOP 5 TIPS

1. 'Firsts' for women are always going to occur in male-dominated professions. Step up and take on challenges that have previously been denied to you, and be those 'first' women to do something new.

2. If someone offers you an amazing opportunity and you are not sure you can do it, say yes and learn how to do it later.

3. You don't need a plan — just roll with the punches as they come along.

4. I believe once you know your WHY, you'll find it easier to know which jobs and which opportunities you should or shouldn't take in your careers. Even if the choices or opportunities are unpopular, if they fit your WHY, it's up to you what you make of them and get out of them.

5. If you need to, you can reset your compass and head in a new direction. Chart your new course now.

Nine

Finding your strengths

We cannot change what we are not aware of,
and once we are aware, we cannot help but change.

Sheryl Sandberg, Chief Operating Officer,
Facebook

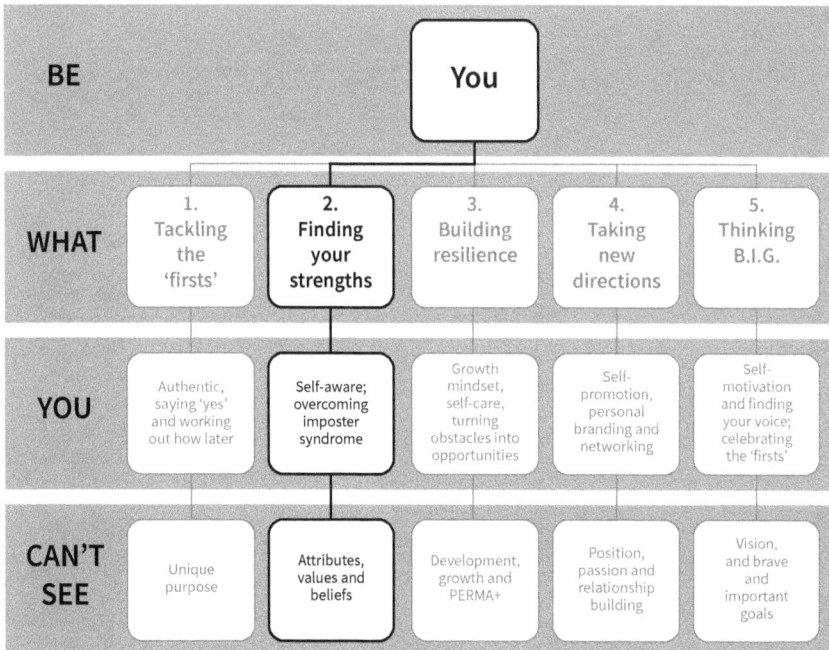

BE		You			
WHAT	1. Tackling the 'firsts'	**2. Finding your strengths**	3. Building resilience	4. Taking new directions	5. Thinking B.I.G.
YOU	Authentic, saying 'yes' and working out how later	Self-aware; overcoming imposter syndrome	Growth mindset, self-care, turning obstacles into opportunities	Self-promotion, personal branding and networking	Self-motivation and finding your voice; celebrating the 'firsts'
CAN'T SEE	Unique purpose	Attributes, values and beliefs	Development, growth and PERMA+	Position, passion and relationship building	Vision, and brave and important goals

The WHAT: Finding your strengths

Now that you know your WHY (discussed in the previous chapter), and you've challenged yourself to be authentic and say yes, you need to know your strengths. I'm not really going to touch on weaknesses or blind spots here, although these are very relevant and knowing them enables you to take steps to change them. Rather, I'm going to focus on strengths and the role they play in the BE-ing and the DO-ing.

Armed with the knowledge of your strengths, you can devise strategies to enhance them and ensure they are directed appropriately to your work, life and other activities. You can think about how you can draw upon them in the complex and challenging situations you might find yourself in your work.

You can use many online tools to find your strengths if you don't know them already, including the Clifton StrengthsFinder or the DiSC profile. You could even use a coach.

Or you could do this very simple exercise. Look through the list of attributes (strengths) shown in the following table. I've also left space for you to add your own. Once you've thought which attributes might apply to you, rate yourself from 1 to 5 (1 being weak and 5 being strong) for each.

	1	2	3	4	5		1	2	3	4	5
Accomplished						Acknowledgement					
Adaptive						Ambitious					
Authentic						Balance					
Bold						Calm					
Collaborative						Compassionate					
Confident						Conscientious					
Considered						Co-operative					
Creative						Curious					
Dedicated						Dependable					
Detail-oriented						Determined					
Diplomatic						Efficient					

	1	2	3	4	5		1	2	3	4	5
Energetic						Ethical					
Fairness						Flexible					
Focus						Freedom					
Friendly						Hard-working					
Harmony						Idealism					
Independent						Innovative					
Kind						Loyal					
Optimistic						Organised					
Passionate						Patient					
Persistent						Practical					
Precise						Professional					
Reliable						Resilient					
Responsible						Resourceful					
Self-starting						Sincere					
Tact						Tenacious					
Trust						Versatile					
Wisdom											

Use your ratings to narrow down your top three attributes and make a note of them here or in your journal (just make sure you write them down!):

1. _____

2. _____

3. _____

These are my top three:

1. Tenacious

2. Resilient

3. Focused

These strengths really supported me during a couple of crucial career points.

Firstly, a staff course I completed in 1993. This was an intensive, six-month, post-graduate level Defence studies course that was a turning point for me. It was the first time I really felt I was in competition with my male colleagues.

On this course, which was based in beautiful Balmoral, NSW, I was one of two Navy women in a class of about forty officers, including national and international officers from across the Army, Air Force and Navy, and some Defence public servants.

I knew I had to be focused and tenacious. I didn't have a bachelor's degree because, when I joined the Navy, that option was not available to women and I had joined straight from school. I was anticipating, and found, a heavy study load—essentially we were completing a twelve-month course crammed into six! I lived on the base from Sunday night to Friday, spending weekends at home in Richmond, NSW, with my then husband who was with the RAAF at RAAF Base Richmond.

I had to be focused, organised and determined. Back then, I felt women had to perform better than the men just to be seen as equals. So, I carefully planned out my study routine, which included starting the major paper—due at the end of the course—at the beginning of the course.

Well, that focus paid off. My other female colleague, Robyn Whitworth, one of the smartest women I knew, and I, were two of the four students to receive an A for that major paper, which were routinely published in the annual *Balmoral Papers* (an official recording of the best papers). At graduation, both Robyn and I were awarded prizes. Mine was the Lonsdale Medallion, for all-round participation, contribution and academics.

But in the face of such success by two women, the only male officer to congratulate us was an international student from Bahrain who, coincidentally, hadn't spoken to us the entire course!

We didn't hear one word from our Australian colleagues. Their ego must have taken a beating.

But this was a true turning point for me. I realised then that I would have to always take a stand for my worth, my value and my achievements. I felt that based on the challenges I had overcome, I deserved my place in this man's Navy.

My resilience and tenacity came to the fore again during my posting to HMAS *Swan* in 1996, which I've mentioned already. Along with the roles I discuss in the previous chapter, this was another example of me again saying yes and working out how later. To be honest, I was shit scared. I didn't have the benefit of prior sea service as a more junior officer, where you learnt the ropes. I was not only in charge of logistics, but I was also the Helicopter Control Officer and Nuclear Biological and Chemical Defence Officer. The former role meant I was responsible for directing helicopters in and out, when they were delivering people or stores, by using hand signals and radio contact only with the bridge of the ship. The latter meant supervising, along with my fellow heads of department, the conduct of exercises involving potential nuclear, biological or chemical attacks, and being able to respond to various scenarios and keep the ship's company safe.

As mentioned, I was one of two women in a crew of 212. The other woman was the Deputy Electrical Engineer, a Lieutenant.

At this time, women were still finding their way at sea, trying to 'lean in' to the environment, living and working in confined spaces, and dealing with the men's negative attitudes towards them. On ships like mine, some structural modifications had been made to take women but, by 1996, it was clear that the age and type of ship was not suited to large numbers of women.

For the women of my time, going to sea was a huge challenge. Many of us were quite senior in rank and age—I was thirty-five years old. We were front-loaded with the kind of training (so we could join our ships) that our male peers received much earlier in their careers. For me, by the time I went to sea, I was at a rank that saw me as one of the senior officers of the ship, part of the executive leadership team.

I wasn't going to be able to fail, to not do my job. My resilience kicked in and didn't let me down. I challenged and overcame the harassment, bullying and intimidation from one of my peers I spoke about earlier in the book. I ensured the ship's company were clothed, fed and paid. The ship maintained its operational schedule because stores were delivered on time—by helicopter, with me standing above the quarterdeck using arm signals to bring it in and out. And, on top of this, we were planning for the ship's decommissioning at the end of the year.

All this ultimately meant the crew conducted numerous exercises and survived! I lived. The crew lived. The ship decommissioned as planned. All with no adverse effects just because the logistics officer was a woman.

Now, let's get back to your strengths.

Once you have a clear picture of your strengths, you can do a few things to make sure you're using them to your advantage.

Own your own development

No matter what specific combination of strengths you have, you will still need to take time to develop skills to help you make the most of them. It's up to you to recognise and identify how your strengths will help you in your career.

You also have to take control of your own development process. No one else will do this for you. This also includes focusing on your key attributes and your values, and what these bring to your organisation.

Don't focus on limitations

If you're the type of person who tends to be self-defeating or to focus on your limitations, you may be tempted to rule out opportunities because you don't feel qualified. Instead of focusing on what you do best, you're mentally preoccupied with your lack of experience, education, or contacts—all of which prevent you from moving forward. (If I had done that, I would never have gone to sea, never challenged myself with something I had never done before, and never had gotten that next promotion.)

Productive, successful people make decisions based on their best qualities and strengths. Focus on what will help you succeed instead of what seems impossible. Have a strong belief in your capabilities, skills and value to your organisation.

Find complementary strengths in others

Focusing on your strengths doesn't mean you should ignore your weaknesses altogether. It just means that you find ways to overcome those weaknesses, and one of the best ways to do this is by leveraging the strengths of others. I found this has worked extremely well in the Navy, which is very team oriented. In fact, Navy's logo has the words 'Navy—The Team Works'. This is because if we can draw on all the strengths of a diverse group, we are stronger, and better able to make quality decisions, consider different perspectives and enhance workplace relations.

Instead of worrying about your shortcomings, find someone with complementary strengths to make up the difference when completing every aspect of your role in your organisation.

Even better, consider your role in the team as a whole and find a position that plays to your strengths and where your weaknesses are irrelevant. Other people within the team can then have the complementary skills for your strengths.

THE YOU: KNOWING WHO YOU ARE

As you gain a firm idea of your strengths, and how you might use these in your organisation and leadership, you are becoming more aware of self, and more aware of who you are BE-ing. And tapping into your Emotional Quotient (or emotional intelligence) is a huge part of being the best version of yourself.

We know that emotional intelligence means the capacity to recognise your own and other people's emotions, and the ability to effectively manage those emotions.

Daniel Goleman, an American author and science journalist, is credited with popularising the argument that non-cognitive skills can matter as much as Intelligence Quotient for workplace success. The following figure shows Goldman's model, where he has separated Emotional Quotient competencies into 'personal' and 'social'. These are further defined by 'recognition' and 'regulation'.

Daniel Goleman's Model

	RECOGNITION	REGULATION
PERSONAL COMPETENCE	**Self-awareness** • Self-confidence • Awareness of your emotional state • Recognising how your behaviour impacts others • Paying attention to how others influence your emotional state	**Self-management** • Getting along well with others • Handling conflict effectively • Clearly expressing ideas and information • Using sensitivity to another person's feelings (empathy) to manage interactions successfully
SOCIAL COMPETENCE	**Social awareness** • Picking up on the mood in the room • Caring what others are going through • Hearing what the other person is 'really' saying	**Relationship management** • Getting along well with others • Handling conflict effectively • Clearly expressing ideas and information • Using sensitivity to another person's feelings (empathy) to manage interactions successfully

All of the competencies shown in the figure are necessary for sound leadership and can be developed if you are lacking in any of them.

But for the purposes of this book, I'm focusing on the personal competency of 'self-awareness', a foundational skill for emotional intelligence.

Self-awareness is commonly described as the capacity for introspection and the ability to recognise oneself as an individual separate from the environment and other individuals. Self-awareness is really just about being aware and confident of who you are BE–ing, but developing your self-awareness helps you learn more about yourself and what you're capable of.

You know how people always say, 'Stay true to yourself'? By becoming self-aware and understanding your strengths and limitations, you open up opportunities that just aren't available otherwise.

Can you see the sequence emerging here?

In the previous chapter, I talked about tackling the 'firsts', being authentic and saying 'yes' to opportunities. I also looked at defining your purpose. You need to know your 'true north' or centre before developing your self-awareness skills.

In this chapter so far, I've looked at strengths and how they help you be who you want to BE, which helps you to say 'yes' to the opportunities. Knowing your strengths and values (which I discuss later in this chapter) are key elements of self-awareness. See how it's already starting to tie in together?

The following sections cover some ways to help you become more self-aware by building on your strengths.

Assess your self-talk

You need to listen to the way you talk to yourself. Do you generally think negative thoughts when you are looking to do something new, complex or challenging, or even something simple? Or maybe you are already a 'Pollyanna'?

Your self-talk will come from your self-beliefs, which include the limiting beliefs you impose on yourself subconsciously. The voices will come; it's how you deal with them that matters, and this defines who you are.

So next time the voices appear, listen to the tone and language. Write them down if you need to, so you can reflect on them later. Then acknowledge the voices, say, 'Thanks, but I don't agree', and repeat to yourself a more positive statement about your ability to do the thing.

This also connects to 'imposter syndrome', which I talk about in more detail later in this chapter.

Use your senses

Your senses (sight and sound, in particular) can provide you with huge insights into your own and other people's feelings and emotions, and situations in general. But these senses are often viewed through the filter of your self-talk.

For example, a frown doesn't always mean that someone's angry, and a groan doesn't necessarily mean that the person you're talking with is bored, despite what your inner voice might be saying.

So, if you feel you are being judged, or being made to feel a certain way about yourself for something you've done, use all your senses and reflect on the spoken words, the tone, the language and the other person's physiology. Ask yourself, 'Could I have misinterpreted what they said or did?'

Tune into your feelings

Of course, tuning into your own feelings is an important element of the personal competency of self-awareness in emotional intelligence. Be conscious of how you are around others. Do you keep your emotions in check? How strong is your sense of self-worth? If it is high, you may already be in tune with your feelings.

If not, maybe you overthink situations and then react in ways you're later apologising for. I know it's not easy because our feelings drive our responses to our experiences. I'm sure you can tap into many examples of how your feelings are expressed in your demeanour, your language — such as clenching your teeth when you're angry or snapping back a response when you feel judged.

If you feel a physical response like this coming on, stop and ask yourself, 'Is this the right response to the situation? Have I misinterpreted anything? How could I respond better in a way that is more compassionate and empathetic?'

Write down your goals, plans and priorities

I cover goals in much more detail in chapter 12, but perhaps you already have a general idea of your overall goals. The important aspect to note here is how your goals connect with your self-awareness and focus. When you have articulated your goals, write them down and plan them out, including smaller actions you can do frequently. This helps you feel less overwhelmed and more focused on you and what you're trying to achieve — to help you move closer to your overall goal.

Ask close and trusted friends and colleagues to describe who they think you are

Ask people you trust for their honest feedback, telling them you are looking for open, honest, critical, constructive and objective perspectives. And then take this feedback openly and without immediately jumping to a response. (Sometimes this is a difficult task for anyone.)

You can then use this feedback from your friends, peers, mentors and colleagues to reflect on how they perceive you and whether this is in alignment with how you see yourself. If, based on the feedback, you wish to change some aspects of your behaviour, make yourself accountable by asking your friends and colleagues to (discreetly) bring it to your attention when they see or hear it.

Practising makes a habit, and you can learn a new habit.

OVERCOMING IMPOSTER SYNDROME

The greatest negative self-talk I hear from women usually emerges when they are offered an amazing opportunity, such as a new job, promotion, or special project. Instead of congratulating themselves, they wonder why they were chosen and if they have the skills, qualifications and competency to do it.

This is imposter syndrome! It's that feeling of, 'I'm an imposter and everyone is about to find out!'

'Imposter syndrome', or rather 'imposter phenomenon', was first documented in the 1970s by American psychologists Suzanne Imes, PhD, and Pauline Rose Clance, PhD. A large amount of research has now been completed in this area, and one of the things this research has highlighted is the twelve signs you might have imposter syndrome. These are:

1. Difficulty accepting praise

2. Discounting own successes

3. Overworking to a fault

4. Compulsion to be the best

5. Perfectionism

6. Fear of failure

7. Avoiding showing confidence

8. Fearing success

9. Focusing on what you haven't done or achieved

10. Being convinced you're not enough

11. Comparing yourself to others

12. Using charm to curry favours

Do any of these resonate with you?

Even Maya Angelou, an American poet, singer, memoirist and civil rights activist, said, 'I have written eleven books, but each time I think … I've run a game on everybody, and they're going to find me out'.

And I too felt this when I was offered a secondment to UN Women HQ in New York in 2016—an opportunity I didn't foresee when I first joined the military over thirty-eight years ago. What for over twenty years had seemed would be a long-term career in maritime logistics transitioned, about ten years ago, almost seamlessly, in to the niche field of gender reform. As I describe in the previous chapter, I moved from one role to the next, from internal gender reform at home in Australia to advising on gender in international military operations in Afghanistan, and from the domestic implementation of government policy on women's roles in conflicts, to advising, guiding and supporting security sector reform in other countries.

Every time I moved to the next job, I wondered when I would get caught out as an 'imposter'. I felt this most intensely when I applied and was accepted for this 2016 secondment with UN Women. In this role, I was providing a military capability to their Peace and Security section, where none had previously existed, and, at the same time, broadening my own knowledge and experience in gender equality and women's empowerment, in ways far beyond my previous roles.

Even with all my previous experience, I wondered whether I really had the necessary background, knowledge and skills to contribute to global interventions and the UN policy on increasing women's leadership and participation, ending violence against women, engaging women in all aspects of peace and security processes, and enhancing women's economic empowerment. I thought, *What gives me the right to be here?*

How did I get to the point of working in New York with a fabulous bunch of women and men, policy specialists, consultants and interns, all of whom have undergraduate degrees, masters and even PhD on topics such as international relations, gender and conflict, human rights and other areas related to our work on women, peace and security?

The terms of reference for the role also required a bachelor's degree. I didn't have one, although during my service I had gained a number of post-graduate qualifications in strategic leadership, resource management, management studies, and administration, and in 2019 I completed a graduate certificate in gender, peace and security at Monash University. Even though I had contributed to academic panels, conferences and publications during my (military) work, I was regularly in awe of the plethora of research papers I saw cross my desk from my UN Women colleagues, which clearly demonstrated their intellectual insights to these issues.

All this made me feel like an 'imposter', and a little inferior. Ultimately, these feelings are a reflection of how little I must have valued my own knowledge and expertise gained as a practitioner, seeing this, in some way, as not being equal to that of my peers.

I took satisfaction in the thought that I probably wouldn't have been selected for this secondment if I wasn't qualified and capable, but nonetheless I wondered when someone would discover I was not who I said I was.

Was I suffering from 'imposter syndrome' or the 'imposter experience'? I prefer the latter, because it describes a phenomenon from which many, if not most, high-achieving women — with high standards, high expectations, and control and perfectionism attributes — suffer. (Perfectionists set excessively high goals for themselves, and when they fail to reach a goal, they experience major self-doubt and worry about measuring up.) The imposter experiences also usually involves procrastination combined with over-preparation for achievement or goal-related tasks, and that sense that 'I must not fail, or I'm just lucky' (as in, to get this job).

The more I read about the research and general symptoms, the more I thought, *Maybe I'm not an 'imposter'*. Research shows that around 70 per cent of people experience the 'imposter phenomenon' so, clearly, I was not alone.

But Richard Branson's advice about saying yes and working it out later rang home. So I just got into the DO-ing of the role. I didn't fail, and I didn't fall over. I started to think, *Maybe I've just got this!*

In fact, taking the role led to many opportunities to share my expertise in gender reform on panels, in conferences, in New York, and around the world. One day, for example, I was delivering training on conflict-related sexual violence to peacekeepers in Jordan, while the next, I was speaking on gender equality in peacekeeping in Abu Dhabi, or developing a gender equality strategy for the defence and security agencies in the Ukraine.

When I finally departed New York in February 2018, the reference provided to me by the Chief of the Peace and Security Section, Paivi Kannisto, included comments such as, 'We have been very privileged to benefit from her expertise and professionalism', 'Jennifer has contributed significantly to the United Nation's work', 'Her unique expertise has been in demand globally' and 'Ms. Wittwer's contribution has been invaluable to UN Women'. This validated my performance and allowed me to give the imposter the flick!

So what can you do about your 'imposter' feelings? Try the following:

- *Accept that you have had some role in your successes and believe in yourself:* You wouldn't be where you are now without the successes, achievements and opportunities along the way that showcase your knowledge and skills, and that you obtained through hard work, study and experience. Knowing your values and strengths and being self-aware contributes hugely to how you value yourself.

- *Speak to your expertise:* You may not know everything on your topic or field of work but talk to what you know. This is what people appreciate about you. At the same time, don't measure yourself by others' 'credentials'. Holding a PhD doesn't mean someone knows more than you, it just means they may have spent more time studying than you.

- *Focus on adding value to collective efforts:* Contributing to group discussions, group work and collective achievements enables everyone's talents and strengths to shine through, and helps you feel like you have contributed to the greater good.

- *Keep a record of the praise you receive:* These are confirmations of your successes, wins and achievements; use them as testimonials for, and affirmations in, your daily work. Don't underestimate the value in receiving, and believing in, praise, and make sure you refer to them when you feel like an imposter.

- *Call out the imposter feelings for what they are:* Tell yourself your mind is a huge reservoir of information that you can rely on when you need it. Stop comparing yourself to others, live and work an authentic life, believe in yourself, and the rest will follow.

Dr Clance (one of the psychologists who first defined this syndrome) also developed the Clance Imposter Phenomenon Scale, which you can use to test yourself against the imposter criteria. You can access it at paulineroseclance.com/pdf/IPTestandscoring.pdf. And you can read more about her research at paulineroseclance.com/impostor_phenomenon.html.

WHAT YOU CAN'T SEE: KNOWING YOUR VALUES AND BUILDING YOUR SELF-BELIEF

Part of finding your strengths is also knowing your core values and having strong self-belief. Let's look at values first.

Understanding the values that matter to you

Values guide your standards or benchmarks and set what you will and won't accept, and what you will and won't compromise on. They provide the roadmap for what's important to you, and guide the way we live our lives and how we make decisions. They are our life's compass.

Do you know your values?

The following provides a list of possible values (again, I've left some space in the list for you to add any values important to you but not listed). Using this list, identify your top ten values—that is, the ones that most resonate for you.

1. Accomplishment
2. Accuracy
3. Acknowledgement
4. Adventure
5. Authenticity
6. Balance
7. Beauty
8. Boldness
9. Calm
10. Challenge
11. Collaboration
12. Community
13. Compassion
14. Comradeship
15. Confidence
16. Connectedness
17. Contentment
18. Contribution
19. Cooperation
20. Courage
21. Creativity
22. Curiosity
23. Determination
24. Directness
25. Discovery
26. Ease
27. Effortlessness
28. Empowerment
29. Enthusiasm
30. Environment
31. Excellence
32. Fairness
33. Flexibility
34. Focus
35. Forgiveness
36. Freedom
37. Friendship
38. Fun
39. Generosity
40. Gentleness
41. Growth
42. Happiness
43. Harmony
44. Health
45. Helpfulness
46. Honesty
47. Honour
48. Humour
49. Idealism
50. Independence
51. Innovation
52. Integrity
53. Intuition
54. Joy

55. Kindness	78. Spirituality
56. Learning	79. Spontaneity
57. Listening	80. Strength
58. Love	81. Tact
59. Loyalty	82. Thankfulness
60. Optimism	83. Tolerance
61. Orderliness	84. Tradition
62. Participation	85. Trust
63. Partnership	86. Understanding
64. Passion	87. Unity
65. Patience	88. Vitality
66. Peace	89. Wisdom
67. Presence	90. _____
68. Productivity	91. _____
69. Recognition	92. _____
70. Resourcefulness	93. _____
71. Respect	94. _____
72. Romance	95. _____
73. Safety	96. _____
74. Self-esteem	97. _____
75. Service	98. _____
76. Simplicity	99. _____
77. Spaciousness	

Circle your top ten values in the list provided here, or write them down in your journal. Next, put a tick next to those values that are essential to your family life, and put a cross next to those values that are important to you in your work life.

From this assessment, distil your top six by looking for the values with both a tick and a cross next to them. Finally, prioritise your core values in order of importance, with the most important first.

All of your top-six values are important, of course, but which are the most important? If you had to choose between two values, which would you fight for, or even die, defending?

Use these thoughts and processes to determine your top three values. Highlight them here or write them down in your journal.

These are my top three:

1. Integrity
2. Courage
3. Grit

And what about your key attributes or strengths that you identified at the start of this chapter? What were the three key personal attributes that you consistently draw upon? The final part to this little jigsaw is realising how you combine your values and attributes to exercise leadership—in your workplace (whatever your role), your home, your community or your relationships.

And so one final activity: select your top two values and two highest scored attributes and provide two examples of how these are reflected in your leadership style. Use the following format for each:

- *Value #1:* _____

- *Example #1:* _____

- *Example #2:* _____

SELF-BELIEFS

And finally (for this chapter at least), to find your strengths and live by your beliefs and values, you need to have a strong sense of self-belief. Self-belief is reflected in the thoughts you have from day to day. These thoughts, whether positive or negative, go to form the thoughts you have about yourself.

Strong self-belief helps you see opportunities, which I discussed in the previous chapter. Add knowing your goals into the mix (and we cover brave and important goals in chapter 12), and you are in the best position you can be to see opportunities, or at least the silver linings in obstacles, and take them. Your self-belief also facilitates creative solutions—and again think, *Say yes and work out how later.* Strong self-belief helps you overcome the anxiety that a new opportunity might bring with it and embrace the unknown and uncertainty.

If you have a high level of trust in your own abilities and the confidence and self-assuredness to know that what you are doing or saying is right for you, you can do anything. Your world will become even bigger if you let go of any limiting self-beliefs and tell yourself, 'I've got this!'

I remember back when I nominated to be part of the team that would take a bunch of young male officer trainees to PNG to trek Kokoda in 1985. As I discuss in chapter 1, no military woman had done this before. And the PNG Army and its bases didn't cater for women at that time. But this didn't even feature in my deliberations about my ability to do it—I thought, *I'm young, fit and well-trained. I've got this.*

But, as I also discuss in chapter 1, the men tried to pull me down with statements along the lines of, 'You're a woman, you can't do this', 'What if you get your period?' and 'There's no separate accommodation for women'—and so it went on.

I don't remember if it was just that I was so confident in myself or that I was completely naïve, but either way, my self-belief held me in good stead. When we finished the trek (after eight days without really washing) and got back to Taurama Barracks in Port Moresby, it was a race to see who got to the showers first. I didn't care. After all, along the way when we came across a swimming hole, I would just strip down to underwear and go for a swim.

The point is I had a heightened sense of self-belief. I believed I could do anything I wanted to. But I have to admit that at times, over the years and depending on the circumstances, this belief did change.

How often have we listened to others, without realising they are just projecting their thoughts and values onto us? How many times have we decided to do or say something even though our intuition told us otherwise?

Think about a time when you gave your power away, when you went against your intuition. What did it feel like? What could you have done differently?

When I was the head of the logistics department on HMAS *Swan* in the mid-1990s, I recall being at sea in a weekly heads of department meeting ahead of a scheduled port visit to the Philippines. Remember, as I shared earlier in this chapter, I was in my mid-30s, this was my first ship posting and, while I was very confident about my logistic responsibilities, I was a little less sure about my other ship roles. The other heads of department were male and quite seasoned sailors. Combined, these aspects made me feel not so self-assured.

Back to the meeting, where we were discussing the forthcoming port visit and when I would open the 'bank' for the ship's company for currency exchanges. (Back then, we still paid our sailors in cash and, as an agent for the Commonwealth Bank, I was authorised to provide currency exchanges in the ports we visited.) I advised what days and times this would occur. The Executive Officer—second in command of the ship after the Captain, but an equal head of department and peer to me—spoke over me and told me when he expected this service to be available.

That little voice in me wanted to say, 'Fuck off, this is my part-of-ship [pardon the pun], don't tell me what to do'. What happened was that I acquiesced to his 'orders'—and then spent the next week at least castigating myself for not standing up to him. I wondered what had happened to that confident young woman who took on her male colleagues and went to Kokoda?

I knew then I had given my power away and decided that it wasn't going to happen again.

Has something like this happened to you? If so, try this little exercise to help you explore your feelings at the time and afterwards. Complete the following sentences:

1. There was a time I gave my power away. It was when …

2. It made me feel like …

3. What I really wanted to do was …

Do this a few more times, writing out your responses in your journal or device. The purpose of this is not to re-live the loss of power, but to re-energise your self-belief through knowing what you really wanted to do, should have done or could do again.

If you feel you give your power away to others just a little too often, here are some tips to get it back:

- *Set important long-term goals but be realistic with them:* Break your goals down into smaller goals, using weekly to-do lists or another system to help you get there in small chunks. Trying to achieve one huge goal in big leaps may set you back if you don't achieve everything you'd hoped—and then you'll feel you have failed and so continue to feed into that limiting self-belief. Small steps will get you there, set you up for success and create more positive self-belief.

- *Stop comparing yourself to others:* I know we women do it all the time. We compare height, weight, make-up, hair, clothing styles, shoes … the list is endless. But we are all unique and if we have positive self-belief and confidence in ourselves, we don't need to compare. While I'm not a fan of Donald Trump, he did say, 'Don't be afraid of being unique. It's like being afraid of your best self.' Step up and own yourself and be proud of that.

- *Develop yourself:* Keep working on personal development. It's not a compliance list—*check, I've done that!* Development is a lifelong process because we list (to use a naval term) sideways[1] from time to time and need to constantly re-balance and get back on course. Besides, it's fun to constantly check in with yourself to see how you are performing!

---

1 The angle of list is the degree to which a vessel heels (leans or tilts) to either port or starboard. A listing vessel is itself stable and at equilibrium, but the distribution of weight aboard (often caused by uneven loading or flooding) causes it to heel to one side.

MY TOP 5 TIPS

1. Armed with the knowledge of your strengths, you can devise strategies to enhance them and ensure they are directed appropriately to your work, life and other activities. You can think about how you might draw upon them in the complex and challenging situations in which you might find yourself in your work.

2. No matter what specific combination of strengths you have, you will still need to take time to develop skills to help you make the most of them. It's up to you to recognise and identify how your strengths will help you in your career.

3. Developing your self-awareness helps you learn more about yourself and what you're capable of. Self-awareness is really just about being aware and confident of who you are BE-ing. Stay true to yourself.

4. Your self-talk will come from your self-beliefs, which include limiting beliefs we impose subconsciously. The voices will come; it's how you deal with them that matters, and which will define who you are.

5. You wouldn't be where you are now without the successes, achievements and opportunities along the way that showcase your knowledge and skills, and that you obtained through hard work, study and experience. Knowing your values and strengths and being self-aware contributes hugely to how you value yourself.

Ten

Building your resilience

The greatest glory of living lies not in never falling, but in rising every time you fall.

Nelson Mandela, quoting 18th-century author Oliver Goldsmith

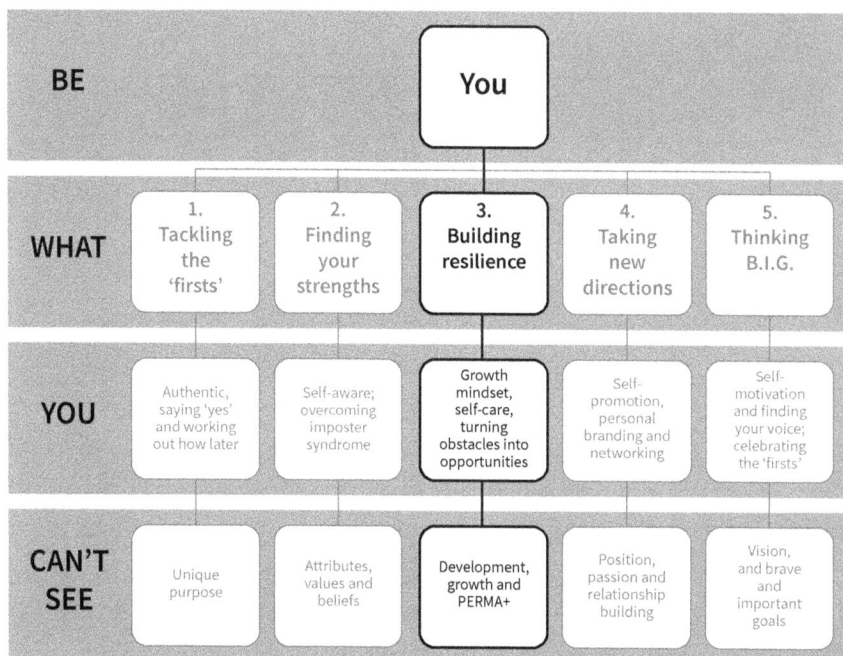

BE			You		
WHAT	1. Tackling the 'firsts'	2. Finding your strengths	**3. Building resilience**	4. Taking new directions	5. Thinking B.I.G.
YOU	Authentic, saying 'yes' and working out how later	Self-aware; overcoming imposter syndrome	Growth mindset, self-care, turning obstacles into opportunities	Self-promotion, personal branding and networking	Self-motivation and finding your voice; celebrating the 'firsts'
CAN'T SEE	Unique purpose	Attributes, values and beliefs	Development, growth and PERMA+	Position, passion and relationship building	Vision, and brave and important goals

143

The WHAT: Building resilience

Have you ever wondered why certain things have happened in your life? Have you ever faced significant challenges in life but not known why? Or why you?

I don't necessarily believe that everything happens for a reason, but I do know that the things that happened to me in my life and my career showed me who I was and, ultimately, who I could be.

In response to everything that happens to you, good and bad, you can ask yourself, 'What is the opportunity for growth? How can I choose to perceive it differently so that I may benefit from the learning?'

Very early on, I learnt my first lesson in resilience, and it was the most significant defining moment of my career. As I mention in chapter 5, during my second year of training, I was raped by a sailor, a fellow member of the Navy.

My resilience for the next 35 years or so came from this incident. I knew if I could survive this, I could get through anything else. I decided then and there I wasn't going to let the bastards get me down. Not the sailor who committed the act, not my superiors if I had reported the incident, and not the court of public opinion (the one that argued because I had drunk too much alcohol it was my fault). I wasn't going to let any of that occur. I pushed it to the back of my mind — not so far that I forgot, but far enough not to let it get in the way. I got on with life and my career, but that little voice was always there in the back of my mind when I faced adversity or challenges again — that one that told me, 'You've beaten them before, you can do it again'.

Perhaps you think I should have faced it head on and reported the incident. However, I felt like I did face it, but in a way that was a win for me. Later down the track, in around 2012, I was able to make a submission to the Defence Abuse Response Taskforce. The Taskforce was established in 2012 to assist complainants who had suffered sexual abuse, physical abuse, sexual harassment and workplace harassment and bullying in Defence prior to 11 April 2011 (this was later extended to 30 June 2016).

As part of that process, I was able to have my complaint investigated by Victorian Police, and while eventually the inquiry was finalised without resolution, I was impressed with the sincerity, support and hard work by the Detective assigned to my case. Investigation and compensation aside, this incident sits with me always, but now, for me, as a proud testament to my resilience and capacity for adversity. Badges of honour really!

But what is resilience?

Humans will often respond in one of two ways to setbacks, trauma, disappointments or obstacles. They will either bounce back, or spiral into hopelessness. If they are able to bounce back they:

- see their situation as temporary

- are optimistic about the future

- exhibit self-belief

- do not blame themselves

- grow from failure

- are tenacious.

If, instead, they are more inclined to spiral into hopelessness, they are also likely to:

- see their situation as permanent

- be pessimistic about the future

- exhibit self-doubt

- blame themselves and others

- be paralysed by failure

- be fearful.

A really good example of resilience, far outweighing what I showed after my experience, was that demonstrated by the Afghan women I met during my deployment to Afghanistan in 2013.

During my time there I spoke with female Army officers, police officers, politicians, shopkeepers, civil servants and students. Some were veterans, others were younger, but all had a story to share. As I mention in chapter 4, one of the meetings I had was with a group of women police officers at Kabul City Police Station. This meeting had been organised for me by Major General Jody Osterman, USMC, who I had mentioned previously as one of my biggest fans — well, in my eyes anyway! Under the watchful eyes of a couple of male Afghan officers, the women and I talked about lots of things, particularly the challenges of working in a male-dominated profession in a Muslim country.

One young policewoman I spoke with was about twenty-four years old. She said she had six children and her husband, also a police officer, had just been killed in a car suicide bombing on the streets of Kabul. Her sad face reflected her grief, but she needed to work, she needed money to support her family. (I wanted to give her a handful of Euros I had in my pocket, but my interpreter cautioned me against this, telling me she would be disciplined if I did so.)

She, like many of the women from this group, was at constant threat of being murdered because, firstly, they were working and, secondly, they were working with men. But along with needing to work to support her family, this woman, again like most of the women I met during my time there, also wanted to be a part of Afghanistan's reconstruction and peace processes.

I met very brave women, day in and day out. Their resilience may be born in conflict, but they are carrying it through to peace.

My research on resilience shows that it generally has four main dimensions:

- *Physical:* In this dimension, fitness and stamina, along with good nutrition and rest and recovery are important areas to focus on.

- *Emotional:* Here, focusing on impulse control and emotional regulation, along with building positivity and realistic optimism can strengthen your resilience.

- *Mental:* Strong self-belief, sustained focus, logical causal analysis and a long-term outlook and perspective are important here.

- *Spiritual:* Here, focusing on your values and beliefs, showing empathy and reaching out for help as needed will build resilience.

You can likely see the inter-relatability of these dimensions with emotional intelligence—strong self-belief, outlook and perspective, emotional regulation, positive emotion, and focusing on personal values and beliefs are all important here as well.

I'm sure building resilience can be achieved in better, more positive ways than what I experienced. You don't have to go through such dark, negative experiences as the women from Afghanistan I spoke with.

The following sections outline three methods that can help.

Pump up the positivity

As the examples through this chapter have shown, emotional strength and finding the positives in negative situations is essential to building resilience.

Research shows that the daily repertoire of emotions of people who are highly resilient is different from those who are not. When not-so-resilient people face difficulties, all of their emotions turn negative. If things are good, they feel good, but if things are bad, they feel horrid.

Resilient people are characterised by an ability to experience both negative and positive emotions even in difficult or painful situations. They mourn losses and endure frustrations, but they also find redeeming potential or value in most challenges.

A key to building resiliency lies in noticing and appreciating those positive experiences whenever and wherever they occur. This often means turning obstacles into opportunities, which I discuss in more detail later in this chapter.

Live to learn

The more you can leverage challenges as opportunities to grow and evolve, the more resilient you are likely to be. Pain comes to all of us in life, we know that. What I see resilient people do, however, is almost immediately look at the problem and say, 'What's the solution to that? What is this trying to teach me?'

Looking at pain as an opportunity to learn and problem-solve — and building the confidence and the habit of moving towards the pain instead of running from it — goes a long way in terms of building resilience.

After I was raped, I asked myself, 'What was the lesson in that for me?' While this was a difficult and painful process, it was a moment of clarity, and of growth and development, for me — that I could use this experience to help other women avoid similar situations, and to help change the culture in which we worked and lived. And I did go on to do that.

Take care of yourself

Good health — and a regular routine of healthy habits — is foundational to both mental and emotional resilience.

When I completed the Kokoda trek in 1986, I was, of course, young and healthy. At the time, I ran cross-country and played volleyball (among other activities) and so I wasn't concerned about the physical training and endurance required to complete the trek.

The experience was more about the mental and emotional resilience I had to build to combat the resistance by the men in the group against my participation.

Have you ever experienced something like this?

Well, like any woman confronted by challenge, and knowing that failure was not an option, the men's claims that I wouldn't last the distance or wouldn't be fit enough were a red flag to a bull. I met all the physical training requirements, I was prepared for the logistic challenges that would arise from being in PNG and, of course, I was keen to show them that I, a woman, could do this.

I learned a lot about human behaviour during that trek. I learned who I could trust and rely on, and who I should avoid. I also hoped that how I met and overcame the challenges when completing this trek would be a lesson to the same young men who doubted my ability to do so.

One example of this was how unwell we all became at different points during the trek, even though we purified our water. My illness came on the last night, as we were perched on Imata Ridge. All we had to do the next day was trek down the ridge, cross the river, climb up the other side and we would be at Owers' Corner, the end of the trek—and there I was with vomiting and diarrhoea all night, no sleep, weak and exhausted. I felt sorry for my tent mates as I retched into a handy garbage bag and had to leave numerous times and dig a hole!

But I got up the next morning, pulled up my big girl pants, secured my backpack, and trudged down the hill. I waded in chest-depth water across the river. And I climbed the last hill, wet, sweaty, vomiting, with no respite. But I did it thinking of our brave Australian soldiers in World War Two, who at that very place not only suffered from sickness, the heat, malaria and whatever else, but were also shooting (and being shot at by) the Japanese.

I felt proud of myself for such an achievement—especially given (as I mention earlier) the young male officer who made the biggest fuss and most derogatory comments about my inclusion on the trek was also sick and allowed another member to carry his pack. I felt I had vindicated myself. I had shown him and the others that I could do this, and that my gender mattered not in these circumstances. I hope he learnt something that day.

I can tell you, it was bloody hard, but it was well worth the pain—physically and mentally. I believe that my ability to remain focused, alert, attuned to my surroundings and confident came from that mental and emotional resilience. It came from a strong sense of self-belief, and the knowledge that true grit is deep inside all of us—you just have to reach in and pull it out.

I had to do this again in 2016, at age fifty-four, when I suffered life-threatening double pneumonia and respiratory failure caused by a bacterial infection. I was intubated and in the intensive care unit (ICU) for five days, on the ward for twelve more and recuperating at home for six months. The doctors told me that my excellent physical condition had certainly played a role in helping my recuperation. Again, however, at times it was emotionally and mentally tough.

This illness struck in full the night before I was due to fly to my long-awaited and dream posting to New York. No surprises perhaps that the day of my flight was Friday 13 May! My illness seemed to come completely out of the blue, and it knocked me for six both physically and mentally.

In the ICU, I suffered from what's been termed 'ICU delirium'. This is an acute and fluctuating disturbance of consciousness and cognition and is a common manifestation of acute brain dysfunction in critically ill patients, occurring in up to 80 per cent of the sickest ICU populations. Yep, that was me.

On the ward, I shared a room with a 95-year-old woman, also with pneumonia, constantly moaning she wanted to die. I was at risk of developing depression. At home, my recuperation was taking so long murmurings started at work that I could be replaced on the posting.

I pushed myself in so many ways to get the medical clearance I needed to proceed on the posting. As soon as I could, I started walking again, first to the letter box and later around the block. I just kept moving. I kept in touch with colleagues to ensure all administration was in place and that my posting remained intact. Finally, in December 2016, I was able to fill the posting.

I believe that my determination in these circumstances came from years of working in a male-dominated profession. In addition, the silver lining that I found in this experience was clarity around what I wanted to do with my life after I returned from New York in 2018. My illness and recovery gave me a clearer picture on where my passion and purpose in life was taking me, which is exactly what I'm doing now.

What does this mean for you? Ensuring that you take care of yourself—physically and mentally—is vital to getting you through the adversity and challenges of life, and helping you look for ways to be grateful for what happens to you in life.

My friend Avril Henry, an Australian expert on leadership, diversity in the workplace and change management (and author of the foreword for this book), fondly says, 'Self-care is not selfish'.

THE YOU: HAVING A GROWTH MINDSET

The concept of 'fixed' (negative) or 'growth' (positive) mindsets was first coined by Dr Carol Dwerk, an American world-renowned Stanford University psychologist who discovered a simple but ground-breaking idea: the power of mindset, and how success can be dramatically influenced by how we think about our talents and abilities.

She said, 'Believing that your qualities are carved in stone—the *fixed mindset*—creates an urgency to prove yourself over and over.' Conversely, in the growth mindset, 'the hand you're dealt is just the starting point for development. This *growth mindset* is based on the belief that your basic qualities are things you can cultivate through your efforts.'

Highly resilient people adapt to new circumstances quickly, are flexible, and thrive in constant change.

Highly resilient people with a growth mindset embrace challenges, view failure and challenges as a chance to learn and grow (remember the 'say yes and work it out later' idea!), have positive thoughts, and see opportunities not obstacles.

Here are some of what I believe are crucial leadership approaches for creating a growth mindset:

- Be open-minded and more inclusive to the unique needs and perspectives of others.

- Be comfortable with ambiguity and uncertainty and don't be afraid to take risks where necessary.

- Utilise the resources and assets of the organisation in ways that guide and drive growth opportunities for yourself and others.

- Accept and promote innovation, change and transformation as a way to help yourself and others succeed.

- Be clear on what you want others to expect from your leadership.

- Take full ownership of yourself; be resilient and don't accept complacency.

- Make opportunities for you and your team to grow together; bring them along on the journey.

- Have a strong leadership presence, which requires self-trust, confidence, self-awareness and emotional intelligence.

- Promote inclusion and individuality to enable rich, innovative and progressive ideas and growth.

- Captivate the heart and minds of your team with vision, purpose and passion.

Turning obstacles into opportunities

There is no such thing as a problem without
a gift for you in its hands.

Richard Bach

An old Zen story tells about a king whose people, he felt, had grown soft and entitled. Unhappy with this state of affairs, the king hoped to teach them a lesson through placing a large boulder in the middle of the main road into the city, completely blocking entry.

Hiding nearby to watch his people's reactions to the obstacle in their way, the King watched as subject after subject came to this impediment and either turned away or, at best, tried half-heartedly before giving up. Many openly complained or cursed the king or fortune or bemoaned the inconvenience, but none managed to do anything about it.

After several days, the story continues, a lone peasant came along the road on his way into town. Instead of turning away or cursing his misfortune, he tied with all his strength to move the rock. Unsuccessful in his attempts, he then ran into the nearby woods, returning with a large branch he then used as a lever to move the rock from the road.

Beneath the rock were a purse of gold coins and the following note from the king:

The obstacle in the path becomes the path. Never forget, within every obstacle is an opportunity to improve our condition.

So in this section, I'm focusing on an important element of the growth mindset: Turning obstacles into opportunities.

Finding the silver lining.

Just BE-ing Pollyanna!

Call it what you like, but for me, the greatest example of this was taking the culture of sexist behaviour towards, and poor treatment of, women in the Navy and carving out a new career in gender reform, starting formally in 2008 (although with roots as far back as 2002). This new career took place over ten years and meant I traversed the globe and other national and international security and defence agencies and organisations.

I'll speak more about this in the next chapter, but essentially, from 2008 on, one opportunity after another led me to Afghanistan, NATO in Brussels, and the UN in New York. While I knew my purpose in 1982 after being raped, and I did pursue opportunities to serve my passion for empowering women in the intervening years, I didn't truly know then what was ahead for me. But as these opportunities emerged, I became what I couldn't see back then.

What have been some of your greatest silver linings? The practice of self-reflection will help create a new positive memory, build on your self-belief, and establish a new behaviour — to always think 'glass half full', rather than 'glass half empty'.

Let's do a small exercise. Think about three initially negative events, decisions or actions you have experienced. Think about how they made you feel, what decisions you made as a result of that, and whether you found a silver lining in that experience.

1. What was the event?

2. What was the silver lining?

Write down your responses in your journal or on your device.

SELF-CARE AND MAINTAINING BALANCE

Of course, focusing on self-care and maintaining work–life balance should not be a gender-specific issue but, in reality, it does seem to affect more women than men.

The two main issues relating to balance seem to be:

- letting go of the guilt (that is, the guilt of spending too much time at work and not enough at home with kids, family and so on)

- learning to say no.

My view is you don't 'find' balance, you 'create' it, and then you decide whether to hold on or let go, depending on context and circumstances.

Creating that balance requires you to define your priorities and values and set some short- and long-term goals around all life areas (see chapter 12 for more information in this area). It requires you to think about expectations, perceptions and attitudes—the 'shoulds' that conflict with your true needs and desires. It requires you to focus on what is important to you, set boundaries around that and not compromise.

A good way for you to assess whether you have the right balance in all areas of your life is to complete a Wheel of Life. This approach is often used in coaching to help people understand where they are currently at, where they would like to be, and how to close the gap between the two.

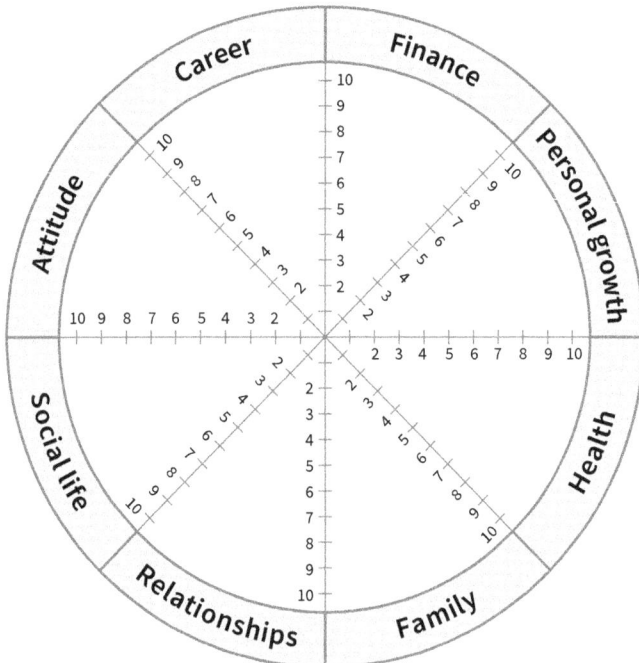

Have a go at this yourself, using the above figure. On a scale of 0 (being the lowest) to 10 (being the highest) put a line to indicate where you are in each particular segment. For example, you may rate yourself as having a whizz-bang social life (10) but as being at a low point (1) in your career. Then, to extend the exercise, use different coloured pens to indicate where you might like to be in twelve months or five years, with the aim being to even out the circle—or make conscious choices about what sections you want your highest ratings to be in. You may even indicate where you were twelve months ago. Once you know where you are and what you want to change, you can set long-term goals and think B.I.G. (see chapter 12).

WHAT YOU CAN'T SEE: GROWING AND DEVELOPING USING THE PERMA MODEL

Research shows that resilience can be taught and measured, with training in resilience being about teaching the psychological skills you need to stop the downward spiral that often follows failure.

If you're not feeling highly resilient in your male-dominated workplace, and struggling with the masculine norm not allowing you to be your authentic self, resilience training can help you in the following ways:

- You can learn to better manage difficult situations and people.

- You're better able to keep your mind on your job and perform well under pressure.

- You can get more done in less time.

- You can achieve your goals.

As I cover earlier in this chapter, emotional and physical wellbeing are paramount to resilience. Dr Martin Seligman, American psychologist, educator and author of self-help books, developed a useful model based on positive psychology research aimed at developing resilience as a skill.

Seligman called it the PERMA model, shown in the following figure.

Positive emotions	Feeling good, optimism, pleasure, enjoyment
Engagement	Finding flow, fulfilling work, interesting hobbies
Relationships	Authentic connections, social connections, love, intimacy, physical interaction
Meaningful	Purposeful existence
Achievement	Sense of accomplishment, ambition, realistic goals, achievement, pride

Dr Seligman suggests that by focusing on the five elements of the PERMA model we can flourish in life and discover happiness.

When you think about it, what I have suggested so far in this and the preceding two chapters conform to this model. Having a purpose, celebrating your achievements, and feeling good even in the face of adversity all fit within this framework. And in the following chapter, I talk about authentic connections and engagement through networking, also a feature of the PERMA model. Of course, I'm not trying to cover off on the vast array of skills you might need in your workplace in this book. I'm merely giving you a sense of how my model sits with already well-developed research and thinking into how you can be the best version of yourself.

So, are you PERMAlicious? If you are, you may just be able to overcome the challenges in your male-dominated workplace with the right mix of resilience, emotional intelligence and a positive mindset. The following figure provides some tips to help you implement the PERMA model into your life and into your workplace.

Positive emotions	• Use your strengths and talents • Be grateful • Spend time with people you care about • Do activities you enjoy • Play with your children, pets and friends • Keep fit
Engagement	• Do what you love • Be mindful • Enjoy the moment • Be fully present • Get back to nature to become more attuned to surroundings • Identify your strengths • Minimise distractions
Relationships	• Make new friends • Be curious about new people • Keep in touch with loved ones • Nurture your relationships • Take time out for yourself • Build positive connections with work colleagues
Meaningful	• Spend time with loved ones • Volunteer • Find your purpose and passion in life • Find and use your strengths • Be authentic, be you, just BE • Work with purpose
Achievement	• Set (SMART) goals • Create your vision • Allow for dream-time • Draw on your strengths and values • Celebrate your achievements • Learn from mistakes and failures

Using the PERMA model and the tips and methods provided, now have a go at thinking how you can use resilience in your leadership in the workplace through completing the following table.

Ten ways to improve your resilience	How it applies in your leadership
1. Find a sense of purpose in your life	
2. Build positive beliefs in your ability	
3. Develop a strong social network	
4. Embrace change	
5. Be optimistic	
6. Nurture yourself	
7. Develop your problem-solving skills	
8. Establish goals	
9. Take action to solve problems	
10. Keep working on your skills	

MY TOP 5 TIPS

1. Resilient people are characterised by an ability to experience both negative and positive emotions, even in difficult or painful situations. They mourn losses and endure frustrations, but they also find redeeming potential or value in most challenges.

2. Looking at pain as an opportunity to learn and problem-solve — and building the confidence and the habit of moving towards the pain instead of running from it — goes a long way in terms of building resilience.

3. A growth mindset is based on the belief that your basic qualities are things you can cultivate through your efforts. Highly resilient people adapt to new circumstances quickly, are flexible and thrive in constant change.

4. Highly resilient people with a growth mindset embrace challenges, view failure as a chance to learn and grow (remember the 'say yes and work it out later' idea!), have positive thoughts, and see opportunities not obstacles.

5. You don't 'find' balance, you 'create' it, and then you decide whether to hold on or let go, depending on context and circumstances.

Eleven

Taking new directions

Simply by sailing in a new direction
You could enlarge the world.

Allen Curnow, from the poem
Landfall in Unknown Seas

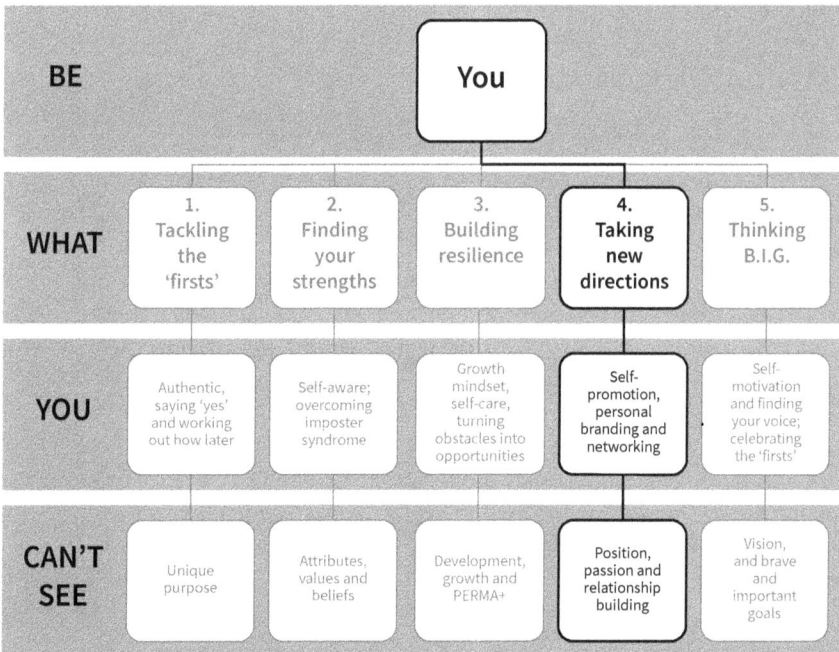

BE			You		
WHAT	1. Tackling the 'firsts'	2. Finding your strengths	3. Building resilience	**4. Taking new directions**	5. Thinking B.I.G.
YOU	Authentic, saying 'yes' and working out how later	Self-aware; overcoming imposter syndrome	Growth mindset, self-care, turning obstacles into opportunities	Self-promotion, personal branding and networking	Self-motivation and finding your voice; celebrating the 'firsts'
CAN'T SEE	Unique purpose	Attributes, values and beliefs	Development, growth and PERMA+	Position, passion and relationship building	Vision, and brave and important goals

Before we look at taking new directions, let's check in and see where we are.

In chapter 7, I introduced you to my Be What You Can't See model, and how you can use this model as a roadmap—or, to put it in naval terms, a chart—to navigating your career in a male-dominated profession.

In chapters 8, 9 and 10, I looked at the first three WHATs of the model: tackling the firsts, finding your strengths, and building your resilience. I've discussed leading authentically as a woman, finding your purpose, or True North, and passions, and saying yes to opportunities even when you don't know how to do it.

I've also outlined how important self-awareness is in knowing who you are and want to be, and how your attributes, values and beliefs will hold you in good stead to overcome imposter syndrome or phenomenon.

And I looked at building resilience through a growth mindset—one focused on growth and development, and turning obstacles into opportunities. With all this under your belt, you're now ready to hold onto your oars as we sail out in new directions—against the wind!

The WHAT: Taking new directions

Turning obstacles into opportunities, which I discuss in the previous chapter, is really what enabled me to take my career in a completely different direction—one that was aligned with my purpose and my passion. And this change in direction came about because of the existing challenges for women in male-dominated professions.

Over the first fifteen years of my time with the Navy, I progressed through the ranks, tackling some major firsts, but also completing some quite routine postings. During these years, as progress was enabling women greater access to occupations and sea service, several incidents occurred that forced the Navy to examine its culture and address sexual harassment and abuse.

In 1993, a female medical officer, posted to HMAS *Swan* (my ship in 1996) made a complaint to Naval authorities alleging she had been raped on board by a senior male officer. He was court-martialled and acquitted, but soon two other women came forward with claims of harassment and discrimination, and a public outcry grew. The ADF conducted an inquiry and, while it found that levels of discrimination were no higher in the armed forces than any other workplace, it highlighted that traditions and behaviour in the previously all-male dominion of the armed forces had to change.

As I outlined in chapter 8, in late 2001, allegations of sexual assault, indecent behaviour and nude sunbathing were made against some sailors from HMAS *Arunta* while vising Diego Garcia in the Indian Ocean. Separate but similar allegations also arose from another ship visit to Christmas Island around the same time.

The ADF has a long history of sexual harassment and sexual abuse, stretching over decades, and the Navy has had its fair share of incidents and allegations. Further incidents since then — and too many to go into here — resulted in an external review of allegations of harassment and abuse in the ADF in 2011, by the then Minister for Defence (ultimately resulting in a report from law firm DLA Piper).

But back to 2002.

It was this existing culture of sexism, harassment and abuse, of which I was a survivor along with many of my women colleagues, that turned my life and career around 180 degrees. It was against the backdrop of change, transformation and progress that I was taking that first step to work for something I was passionate about and which served my purpose.

The existing culture was the *obstacle*.

I also mention in chapter 8 that I was selected to be a part of the inquiry team to travel to Diego Garcia in January 2002 and conduct a quick assessment of the allegations. (I run through the same time line of events in my career in the remainder of this section as I do in chapter 8, but my focus here is on the opportunities and new directions taken.)

On my return to Canberra, I found the Navy had created a role to examine its organisational culture and they appointed me as the inaugural director. It was time to review the Navy's values, its mission, and what it meant to serve.

This was the *first* opportunity.

I left this role in 2004 for a period of Reserve service (for greater flexibility with my daughters at school) but returned to it in 2008 because no one else wanted to do it.

This was the *second* opportunity.

This time round, I was well supported by my (male) Navy leadership, who supported and funded my ideas to develop women's mentoring, networking and leadership programs. And I'm proud to say these programs continue to this day.

This tentative step by the Navy in 2008 ultimately paved a smooth path for the implementation of Elizabeth Broderick's review into the treatment of women in the ADF in 2012. But in between, in 2009, the Navy embarked on an ambitious flagship cultural reform agenda — NGN — and I was asked to join the team appointed to develop and implement the reform agenda.

The *third* opportunity.

A number of projects were approved as part of these reforms, including one that examined opportunities for increasing (gender) diversity and inclusion, and that, of course, fell to me.

As NGN progressed and the team grew, over time it became clear that significant effort was needed to deal with matters associated with the retention, development and advancement of women in the Navy. This was in part due to changes through NGN, as well as the requirement within the Navy to meet its commitments to an ADF–wide initiative to address women's recruitment and retention (titled the Chief of Defence Force Action Plan for the Recruitment and Retention of Women in the Australian Defence Force).

And the Navy created a new role for me as a women's strategic adviser and women's advocate for the Navy's senior leadership team.

The *fourth* opportunity.

It was in this role in 2012 that I first connected with NATO in Brussels for their annual military committee meeting on gender perspective, and it was here that I first learnt about the role of gender advisers in NATO military operations in Afghanistan and Kosovo.

I stayed connected to this committee for six years in the various roles I subsequently assumed and later, it was at this committee where we could share the ADF's implementation of the Broderick Review, so that other countries might benefit from our experience and responses.

Wait, there's more. My *fifth* opportunity.

I came back to Australia after the conference in June 2012 ecstatic about the role of gender advisers in NATO operations, but truly thinking that this would never transpire for an Australian military officer (the Scandinavians had held the fort for some years).

But only a month later, my boss, the then Deputy Chief of Navy, Rear Admiral Trevor Jones, RAN told me I would be filling the gender advisor role in Afghanistan.

Personally, this was a significant achievement. I was getting to deploy not only to a land operation (I talk about the issues of joining a peacetime Navy in chapter 1) but also into a role that I was very passionate about. And this role afforded me the opportunity to learn more about women's progression in other armed forces and security agencies, and how NATO was supporting the recruitment and retention of women.

Then, the *sixth* opportunity. I know, they just keep on coming. (Third last one, I promise!)

While I was away on deployment, implementing NATO's policy on women, peace and security, back home, they were creating (yet) another position for me—this time to lead the implementation of the Australian Government National Action Plan on women, peace and security.

I was still the only officer with the necessary knowledge, skills and experience, so I was promoted to Captain rank to fill the role, and was privileged to work directly to the CDF and his generals.

Then came the *seventh* opportunity.

My last posting in the Navy was with UN Women HQ in New York in 2016. This secondment was an initiative of our National Action Plan and I had, in fact, written the duty statement for the position—selfishly, of course, to match my qualifications and experience!

This was such an exciting time for me. I wasn't really in the role in my military capacity, but as a policy specialist on peacekeeping (including women's participation and sexual violence in conflict) and sexual exploitation and abuse. While UN Women's offices were on 220 East 42nd Street, I was attending meetings, conferences and workshops in the hallowed halls of the UN building quite regularly.

The experience was truly awesome, full of many arm-pinching moments. I mentioned my feelings of imposter syndrome during this time in chapter 9. But it was my experiences with UN Women that ultimately led to my final — *eighth* — opportunity.

My exploits around the world as I represented UN Women at various forums and trainings meant that I grew my international network of colleagues from armed forces, government organisations, non-government organisations, think tanks, civil society groups, academics and activities. I had built up a lot of goodwill with NATO and the UN and was able to draw upon this later to facilitate UN Women's work.

One of the major activities that I was involved in was providing military expertise to the UN Women team in Ukraine, who were supporting government-sponsored gender reform in the Ukraine defence and security agencies. My job was to review and analyse first a gender impact assessment and then a gender equality strategy, to ensure the strategy reflected recommendations that would be consistent with other international approaches to reform in these sectors.

I took the time to develop and nurture relationships with my Ukrainian colleagues across the UN, the armed forces and the police. Similar to during my time in Afghanistan, I developed a fondness for a country that is slowly but confidently emerging as a new Eastern European country. The language sounds harsh, the public sometimes not so friendly, and not many speak English, but I connected with my colleagues.

And so, in a roundabout way, this led to my eighth and final opportunity.

When I returned to Australia from New York in 2018, I knew I had nothing left to offer the ADF. I had performed in the most senior role possible in the niche field of women, peace and security. I knew I wanted to keep working in this space.

So, the only possible outcome was to leave full-time service and become an international consultant. And, because of all my past opportunities and experiences, and the services of a wonderful business coach, Amanda Cromer, I felt fully prepared to leave and carry on my work.

Of course, I thank the ADF for handing me these amazing eight opportunities, one after another, that not only helped to build a new niche capability in the ADF, but also gave me the skills, qualifications and experience to branch out on my own.

And I did.

I contracted back to UN Women in Ukraine in 2018 to develop a strategic training framework on gender and women, peace and security for the Ukrainian armed forces.

I contracted to the Peace Operations Training Institute (POTI) in the US to re-write a course on preventing violence against women and promoting gender equality in peacekeeping.

And, as I write, I've just embarked on a two-year contract with UN Women in Jordan to implement their national action plan on women, peace and security into their defence and security institutions. And I'm also completing more work with POTI re-writing three women, peace and security courses.

I know this has been a long(ish) rundown of all the opportunities throughout my career, but I wanted to show you how one opportunity led to another, how I took advantage of each one, although they were new roles, and how important they became to establishing myself in a new career path, a different direction.

You can do this, too.

In the following sections, I outline some of the ways you can support yourself as you navigate your new direction. I found some of these came naturally for me, and some I had to develop. But they are all important elements of BE-ing the best version of yourself.

THE YOU: SELF-PROMOTION

I think women experience more difficulty with self-promotion than men. Many don't know how to promote their skills, knowledge and expertise without feeling others are judging them, being seen to be bragging, or falling foul of the tall poppy syndrome.

Do you feel like this?

Perhaps you also work in a team and organisation where the culture leans more towards team rather than personal recognition. Nothing is wrong with this of course, but at times, in my humble opinion, you need to own and be acknowledged for your achievements.

Research shows that women fail to get promoted because they fail to step up and let their superiors know what they have done and what they have achieved. They sometimes think that their achievements will speak for themselves. Is this what you believe?

A relevant example of this is Sharon Allen, who was appointed chair of Deloitte and Touche USA in 2003. She was, at that point, the highest-ranking woman in the firm's history and also the first woman to hold that role within that industry. But she'd learnt some lessons along the way. Importantly, she describes learning how detrimental not using your voice and self-promoting was to your career.

In her thirties, she says she was shocked to discover she hadn't made the cut on a round of promotions. She confronted her boss, outlined what she had done and why she deserved promotion. Her boss responded, 'I had no idea, you didn't let me know'.

Marketing yourself as a valuable commodity or seeing yourself as valuable outside of your team shouldn't feel uncomfortable.

Perhaps you don't want to draw attention to the fact you are a woman. Perhaps it's a confidence issue. As I talk about in chapter 3 (and at other points through this book) maybe you'll go to great lengths to avoid attention, to blend in, to become 'beige'.

On International Women's Day in 2019 Australia's prime minister uttered some very disappointing words: 'We want women to rise but not at the expense of others' (meaning men). Once again we were back to the 'equity pie' idea I talk about in chapter 2, as if more rights for women somehow means fewer rights for men (once again, it's not pie!). These types of comments continue to highlight that women still need to remain confident and assertive in the face of these challenges, attitudes and perceptions.

Self-promotion is a leadership competency that is essential for communicating your talent and establishing your credibility. The following figure shows the main elements to focus on in the process.

Human qualities	Personal value proposition	Talents/ performance	Personal brand	Self- promotion
Values, attributes, passions	Achievements, current impact, future contributions	Credibility, reputation	Strengths, values, passions, purpose	Story telling, and *story showing*, in an authentic way

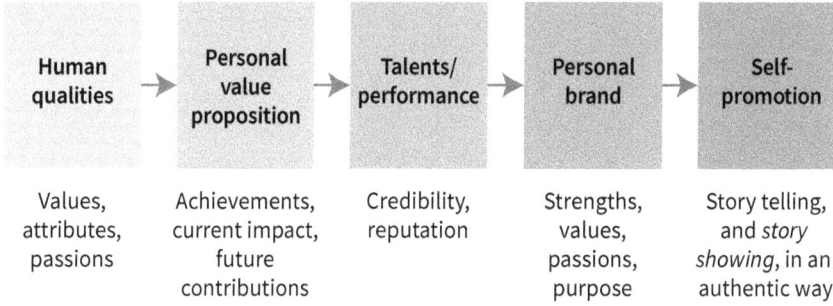

Self-promotion is about the art of telling and showing your story in an authentic way.

In *The Art of Self Promotion: Tell Your Story, Transform Your Career*, American author and executive coach Debby Stone says you need to *tell* your story to transform your career. She shares a great example of 'telling' a (self-promotion) story that made the audience laugh, but also meant she shared her credentials without being boring and she engaged them. She then circled back so that she ended where the story began.

A different approach is offered by Australian entrepreneur Sam Cawthorn. In *Storyshowing: How to stand out from the storytellers*, he takes the concept of self-promotion further. Sam believes personal stories (and his own begins with a life-changing event in 2006) have the power to inspire, influence and motivate (and, hell, isn't this why we tell our story?) but that often the stories fail to deliver on this because of the *way* they are told. His mantra is, 'If you want your stories to lead to action, it's time to stop telling them and to start showing them'. I highly recommend this book if you are considering getting into public speaking; I guarantee it will inspire you to change your approach to telling your story.

So, ultimately, it is up to you how you 'tell' your stories about your achievements, success, wins, failures, obstacles. But if you want to impress, influence or change another woman's life, also know how to 'show' your story.

The preceding figure is my model of self-promotion. Working from left to right of the model:

- You need to know who you want to BE.

- You need to know, and believe in, your value to the organisation.

- Performance is not everything, but your achievements help with your credibility and reputation, so own them.

- If you know who you are, you can brand yourself.

- If you brand yourself well and authentically, you can tell your story authentically.

And, by the way, no one is Robinson Crusoe. One of the myths about self-promotion is that it means to advocate just for oneself. But speaking about your team's accomplishments is another effective way to expand your own leadership and gain visibility. By doing so, you indirectly showcase your judgement, decision-making skills, and contributions while you promote others.

Debby Stone also talks about the fundamentals of self-promotion—and what it is and what it isn't. (And I highly recommend her book to help you allay any fears you might have about self-promotion.) The following table summarises Stone's tips for what self-promotion is and isn't.

What self-promotion IS	What self-promotion IS NOT
Telling your story	Selling yourself
Being authentic	Putting on a persona
Being positive	Disparaging others
Displaying confidence	Being arrogant
Showcasing your strengths	Bragging
Highlighting your accomplishments	Oversharing and overpowering
Establishing your credibility	Regurgitating your résumé
Creating curiosity	Reciting a boring, canned speech
Leveraging your experiences	Embellishing the truth

So forget the 'tall poppy syndrome'! Forget the judgement of others. Make self-promotion an important part of your leadership toolkit.

Personal branding

Many women (and probably men) are not sure they need personal branding if they are working for someone else, or in a large industry—like the military for example.

But your personal brand matters.

Your brand is your reputation. Your reputation is your brand. It's your calling card. It's what you're known for and how people experience you. It's about bringing who you are to what you do and how you do it (and fits in beautifully with the Be What You Can't See model).

This is my brand:

I am a professional but very unique woman who is passionate about supporting women and empowering them to be the best they can be. I inspire and motivate women to be courageous and use their voice. I am a trusted and credible mentor and coach and I serve with integrity, courage, meaning and purpose.

I like to think that if you ask anyone to describe who I am, words similar to these would come to mind.

What do people say about you?

Delivering your brand clearly and consistently will create a memorable experience in the minds of those you interact with. And this can open doors to new opportunities.

So how do you brand yourself? I have three tips:

1. Firstly, have clarity around your attributes, values, beliefs, passions, vision (which I cover in the following chapter), mission, skills, expertise, knowledge, accomplishments ... the list goes on—just about everything I've covered in part II of this book!

2. Then, communicate all of these into every type of communication you produce, including your conversations, engagements, interactions and behaviour.

3. Finally, capitalise or leverage these to be able to do what you want in a way that is known, respected, valued and appreciated. This means accepting speaking invitations, conducting workshops, writing articles and blogs, and using social media to share issues and your opinions. This will help you slowly build not only your credibility as an expert, but also your brand and reputation.

But perhaps a word of caution here: you may have a number of passions; they may be unrelated and varied. My experience is that when building your brand and credibility, focus on the one passion that gets you up in the morning. The one you care most about, the one you want to make a living from. If you try to cover too much ground, you may get lost, those you are trying to reach may get confused, and you run the risk of losing them. For me, I have never faltered from my passion and purpose in being an advocate for women's equality, rights and empowerment. I keep my public comments and opinions focused on this domain—even though, of course, many social issues catch my eye!

Effective networking

What do you really think networking is all about? Again, some people think it's just about selling yourself or regurgitating your résumé. Instead, it's about building trustworthy and reliable relationships, communicating passions and connecting with people—not collecting people.

You can become truly empowered through being known as a powerful resource—giving not taking—and knowing who you are and what value you can add.

The following figure outlines my top tips when networking.

Ask yourself what your goals are in participating in working meetings	Visit as many groups as possible that spark your interest	Hold volunteer positions in organisations you're passionate about
Ask open-ended questions in networking conversations	Become known as a powerful resource for others	Have a clear under-standing of what you do, why, for whom, and what makes your doing it special or different
Be able to articulate what you are looking for and how others may help you	Follow through quickly and efficiently on referrals you are given	Call those you meet who may benefit from what you do and vice versa

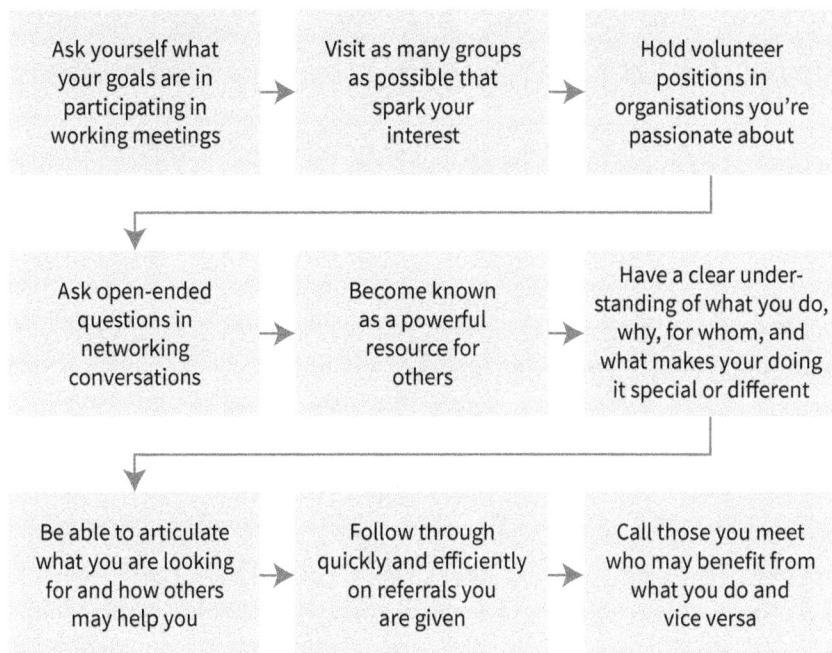

The 'elevator pitch'

And, of course, when you're networking, the art of self-promotion and storytelling/showing comes to the fore—and most intensely so when delivering your 'elevator pitch'.

Do you have such a pitch crafted, practised and ready to deliver? Do you even know what one really is?

The elevator pitch is a brief, persuasive speech that you use to spark someone's interest in you. A good pitch should last no longer than 20 to 30 seconds, roughly the time it takes to go up a few floors in a lift (hence the name). Your elevator pitch should be interesting, memorable and succinct. It also needs to explain what makes you unique.

It can take some time to get your '30 seconds of me' pitch right, so you'll most likely go through several versions before finding one that is both compelling and sounds natural in normal conversation.

This is not where you might say, 'Hi, I'm Captain Jennifer Wittwer, I'm the Director … blah, blah, blah … I worked … blah, blah, blah'.

What people want to hear me say is, *'Hi, I'm Jennifer. I help organ-isations address the challenges of women's participation and representation in the workplace and empower women to take leadership roles and reach their full potential. I do this through consulting, coaching and mentoring. What are some of your challenges and what do you do to overcome them?'*, or words to that effect.

And, while we're looking at forums where short and snappy is best, the same is true for platforms such as LinkedIn. Here too you need to craft a statement—an elevator pitch—that talks to who you are, what you stand for and what you do.

The following figure outlines the elements of an elevator pitch.

1. Identify your goal

This is the objective of the pitch—for example, to sell a product or tell clients about your organisation.

2. Explain what you do

Focus on the problems you solve and how you help people. Add information that shows the value of what you do.

3. Communicate your personal value proposition (PVP)

Outline what makes you, your idea or your organisation unique.

4. Put it all together

Ensure the whole pitch lasts for 20 to 30 seconds (between 50 and 75 words).

5. Practice

So, if you don't have an elevator pitch already, let's create one.

First, simply answer the following questions:

- What do I do?

- What do I want to do?

- What achievements am I most proud of?
    1.
    2.
    3.

- What inspires me about my work?

- What sets me apart?

Once you've included your answers to these questions in your pitch, engage at the end with a question. The elevator pitch is designed to draw a person into conversation, so it's important that when your 20 or 30 seconds are up, you invite the other person to speak. Preparing a few standard open questions (that is, those that can't be answered with a 'yes' or 'no') to use at the end of your pitch will usually do the trick.

Now, review what you've written, ensuring your final statement is around five sentences, and hone it until it sounds natural and compelling—and then practise it.

WHAT YOU CAN'T SEE: POSITION

Jemimah Ashleigh, a young Australian entrepreneur and small business owner, published a book in 2018 on the importance of positioning in the marketplace. Like me, she also espoused the notion of saying yes and figuring the details out later as she moved from public service work into her business, and she definitely learned that failure will not kill you.

While she talks about positioning in terms of business, her ideas are congruent with positioning yourself in the workplace and becoming known as an expert in your field. She makes numerous good points, which I outline here, along with my take on her arguments:

- *Your job is to do your job, not explain it to everyone else:* I say, this is true, and you do not need to explain yourself, your actions or your plan to anyone else other than those you might want to help you keep accountable to your goals.

- *Don't be scared to leave the party:* I say, if your situation is not allowing you to be true to yourself, or to be authentic, then find somewhere else where you will be valued and appreciated. Life is too short.

- *When someone fucks up, it's not your fault and it's not your problem:* I say, you are not responsible for everyone else. Negotiate some compromises if you need to, but don't give in when they try to make their issue your issue.

- *You have to fall before you can fly:* I say, making mistakes and failure is part of life, learning and the journey. Use your resilience and strength to bounce back and own your actions. Falling over and getting back up will help you fly.

- *Alignment is when all the things you have been doing and what you are meant to be doing comes together:* I say, this is when you have created your vision, set your B.I.G. (see following chapter), put your action plan in place, and chartered your new course. Now you're sailing!

Ashleigh also talks about authenticity, personal branding, stopping the negative self-talk, mentoring, networking—all things I've covered in this chapter and throughout the book. So if I've said it, and she's said it, it must be true, right?

Passion

One thing I have found so important to position yourself and being what you can't see is having a passion and acting on it. I've already told you my story on what really fired up my passion earlier in the book. I definitely don't recommend this as a development method, but of course we can't necessarily stop some things from happening. And as I've also said, it's about turning that obstacle around and into an opportunity.

I believe having a passion and pursuing it is at the very heart of our levels of satisfaction, joy, love and happiness. The Cambridge

Dictionary defines passion as 'a very powerful feeling, an extreme interest in or wish to do something'. And this is how it should be for the one thing that drives you to do what you do.

Because of my early experiences, my passion has always been to support and lift up other women. I've done this throughout my military service by coaching and mentoring my subordinates, training as an Equity Adviser to advise and support women who have experienced inappropriate conduct by others in the workplace, and training for and learning about how conflict and war affects women and girls so I could advocate for them and enable policy changes. I've done all this by tacking from port to starboard across a number of roles that were designed to make a difference for women.

In my life as an international consultant and military reservist, I continue to coach and mentor women, I help other armed forces develop their policies and systems relating to women's representation, and I undertake Reserve service only on gender-related programs and initiatives. I set sail early in my career and have not diverted from this course (even when it was against the wind of accepted practice).

This passion has been behind every opportunity I took, every decision I made, every action that enabled me to become what I couldn't see.

What is your passion?

Your passion isn't necessarily your job. I loved that I was able to combine both, but the same doesn't necessarily have to be true for you. If you haven't yet found your passion, here are some simple ideas to help you:

- *Expand your perspective:* Get out and see the world. This may be in a literal sense, such as through travel, or metaphoric, such as through stepping outside your comfort zone and doing something different.

- *Let your pain be your purpose:* As I have previously described, my purpose or passion was born from pain. Think about what you have struggled with in your life, how you overcame these struggles, and then what you can share with others to alleviate their same pain.

- *Reconnect to your inner child:* Remember what you did before you imposed boundaries and conditions on your life. What did you love doing? When did you feel most free? What gave you joy?

- *Spend time in silence:* My wonderful coach, Amanda Cromer, once asked me to sit for ninety minutes each day and do nothing. No reading, writing or watching TV. Just nothing. She suggested this because I was always on the go, my mind was moving faster than Superman, and I wasn't taking life in. But ninety minutes? I said she was crazy. I tried ten minutes because this was more achievable. And she was right. The time helped me reconnect with me. It helped me to think. I never got to ninety minutes but the seed was planted!

- *Spend time with others who share the same interests as you:* Be with people who lift you up, don't put you down. Life is too short.

- *Give to something that is bigger than yourself:* Be philanthropic, and find joy in helping or giving to others. Learn how to measure your circumstances against others (in a positive way) and put your life, desires, passion and vision in perspective. Doing so will give you more clarity.

Relationship building

And, finally for this chapter, relationship building is so important to your professional and personal development, positioning yourself in your work, and achieving your vision and B.I.G. (see next chapter).

When I arrived in Kabul in January 2013 as the Gender Adviser, with the task of integrating gender perspective into the plans and operations of the NATO joint command, I was on my own. My position was embedded in a small civil-military team, located within one division of the command, and functionally isolated from those with whom I needed to work (the plans and operations people).

I was pretty much left to my own devices, because no one really understood how 'gender' fitted in to 'war'. I realised very early on that the way to smooth my path was to build relationships with the key people I needed on my side—and I knew who they were. First was my Colonel, (Kendall Parks, US Army) so he would give me the space and flexibility I needed to create the necessary framework to embed the NATO gender policies. Next was the Chief of Staff to the Joint Commander, so I could persuade him that I needed to be part of the command team. (I achieved this at the three-month mark!)

Then I had the two Generals heading up the Plans and Operations Divisions, because these were the main areas I need to affect with my work. I've mentioned them a couple of times, such influence and impact they've had on me; General Gus McLachlan, an Australian Army officer, and Lieutenant General Jody Osterman, USMC, the latter being easily influenced by my charm and supply of Tim Tam biscuits! In all seriousness, these were two senior officers who understood the importance of gender perspective, appreciated my professional ethic and purpose, and easily facilitated the integration of my work within their areas of responsibility. (If you're interested in reading about Gus's gender journey in Afghanistan, check out *Women, peace and security: reflections from Australian male leaders*, published by the Australian Civil Military Centre in 2015 and accessible at www.acmc. gov.au/resources/publications/women-peace-and-security-reflections-australian-male-leaders.)

But the important point is that I took the time to get to know them, to educate them on NATO's gender policies, and to explain how my efforts could affect and enhance the planning and conduct of operational activities. I attended their meetings, talked to their staff and kept them informed. For their part, they were open to new concepts, inviting me to be part of their key information and decision forums, and giving me authority to work within their divisions, carte blanche. This was because they respected and trusted me, based on the relationship I had built with them.

I found this approach had worked for me many times as I worked for senior officers, and my results spoke for themselves. Navy Admiral Davyd Thomas would, as Deputy Chief of Navy, wander down to my office to talk about funding for women's leadership programs. Admiral Trevor Jones, who also was at one time the Deputy Chief of Navy, gave me the opportunity, space and support to develop a key women's advisory role and work with him directly on matters affecting women's service. Air Marshal Mark Binskin, as CDF, in 2013 said,

'Implement the National Action Plan on women, peace and security,' and then he let me just get on and do it!

I have too many more examples to share here, but you get my drift.

Take the time to identify your key stakeholders. Make appointments so you can talk to them about what you do, what you want to do and how you will do it. Keep them posted on your progress. They will come to trust you implicitly to achieve their results or the outcomes you're looking for.

I found that by doing this, I remained true to my charted course.

MY TOP 5 TIPS

1. You may work in a team where the culture leans more towards team rather than personal recognition, but at times you need to own and be acknowledged for your achievements.

2. Self-promotion is a leadership competency that is essential for communicating your talent and establishing your credibility. It's the art of telling your story in an authentic way.

3. Speaking about your team's accomplishments is another effective way to expand your own leadership and gain visibility. By doing so, you indirectly showcase your judgement, decision-making skills and contributions while you promote others.

4. Your brand is your reputation. It's your calling card. It's what you're known for and how people experience you. It's about bringing who you are to what you do and how you do it.

5. Networking is about building trustworthy and reliable relationships, communicating passions and connecting with people — not collecting people.

Twelve

Thinking B.I.G.

*You cannot change your destination overnight,
but you can change your direction overnight.*

**Jim Rohn, American entrepreneur,
author and motivational speaker**

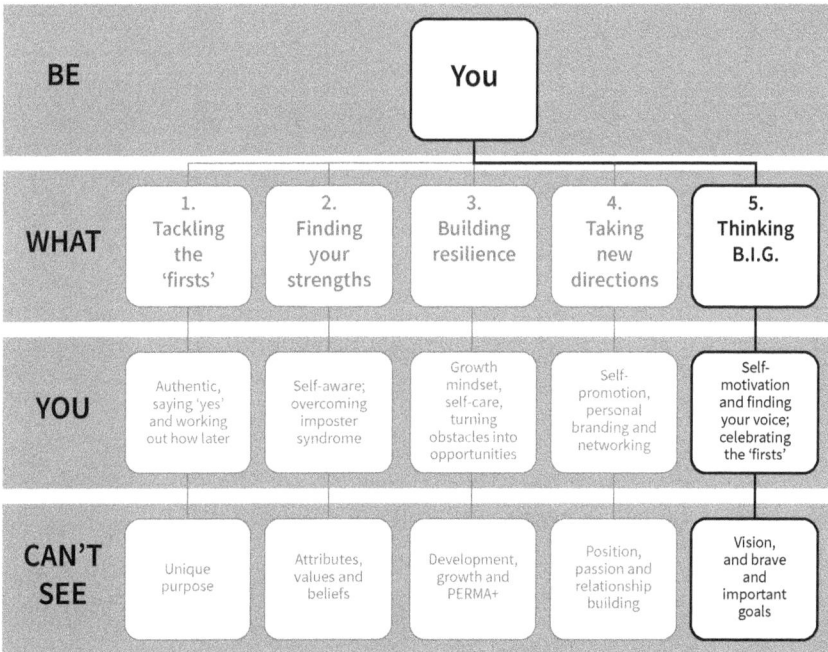

BE			You		
WHAT	1. Tackling the 'firsts'	2. Finding your strengths	3. Building resilience	4. Taking new directions	**5. Thinking B.I.G.**
YOU	Authentic, saying 'yes' and working out how later	Self-aware; overcoming imposter syndrome	Growth mindset, self-care, turning obstacles into opportunities	Self-promotion, personal branding and networking	Self-motivation and finding your voice; celebrating the 'firsts'
CAN'T SEE	Unique purpose	Attributes, values and beliefs	Development, growth and PERMA+	Position, passion and relationship building	Vision, and brave and important goals

The WHAT: Thinking B.I.G.

The quote from Jim Rohn at the start of this chapter provides a perfect transition from the last chapter (which focused on new directions) to this one—which is all about thinking B.I.G.—brave and important goals.

We have just about nailed the Be What You Can't See model, and this is the last WHAT. Here I'm asking you to think about where you want to be in five, ten and twenty years, whether in your current profession or another. I'm asking you to think about what you can do now to position yourself to meet those goals. This means taking a longer term view of your career, not one focused on a short-term gain or fix.

We all know that setting goals is important to our purpose, our work and our lives. Without them, do we really know what we are aiming for in life?

Throughout this book, I've talked about the importance of creating a vision for who you want to BE, what you need to DO, and what you want to HAVE. I'm going to talk about how this connects to thinking B.I.G. a little bit later in this chapter. But let's start with the DO-ing for this fifth element of the model—self-motivation, finding your voice and celebrating the 'firsts'.

The YOU: Self-motivation

One of the most challenging things for women in male-dominated professions and workplaces is remaining self-motivated. Self-motivation in its simplest form is the power that drives you to keep moving ahead. It encourages learning and development (and building resilience along the way) and is a primary means to achieving your goals.

I cover emotional intelligence in chapter 9, including the way Daniel Goleman includes self-motivation (or self-management) as a key personal competency along with self-awareness. Indeed, the emotional intelligence competencies Goleman outlined connect with many aspects of my model—BE-ing in tune with, and attuned to, your emotional competencies makes it highly likely you can be what you can't see.

Self-motivation is about the ability to do what needs to be done, without influence or supervision from other people or situations. People with self-motivation and with high levels of resilience can find a reason and strength to complete a task even in the face of adversity or in the absence of any support.

I know that had I not been self-motivated in the first few years of my career, I would not have made it. If I had given into the effects of that sexual assault, the constant sexual harassment, the intimidation and bullying, I wouldn't have achieved my dreams.

Let me give you another specific example. In 1990, when my initial nine-year commission was about to expire, I was offered a permanent commission. I was a Lieutenant and working at the Navy apprentice training establishment, HMAS *Nirimba*, in Sydney. At the same time, I had just been given a task by the commanding officer, who wanted a childcare centre built on the base to cater for Navy women, because, at that time, they were reluctant to return to work after maternity leave due to the unavailability or lack of good childcare.

Oh, okay, I'll just build a childcare centre because I know everything about that, I thought. But I agreed—I suppose another example of saying yes and working it out later. The commanding officer gave me a demountable building and funding; I think it was about $100,000.

Well, about a year later, the Little Pelicans Child Care Centre, the first fully licensed childcare facility on a Navy base, was opened. It had been a monumental task—during which I was also doing my day job as a logistics officer—where I started with research and ended with becoming president of the association that would manage the centre. And, of course, everything else in between.

I was motivated to do this—partly because I had been given an order, and my response was, 'Yes Sir!' and partly because it meant I had to accept the permanent commission to stay on and finish the job. But another large motivator was that it aligned with my purpose to support and empower women. And the offshoot of this was making the decision to remain in the Navy because I felt I had more to do.

And now, with time passed, I can say that's true.

I wonder how self-motivated you feel in your current position and workplace. Are you energised, passionate and full of life? Or not so happy because you feel like you don't quite fit and don't know how to be your authentic self?

Are you motivated enough to achieve what you really want in life? Because wanting to do something and actually motivating yourself to do it are two different things.

Research shows that four factors are necessary to build the strongest levels of self-motivation:

- *Self-confidence and self-efficacy:* This is a belief in your ability to succeed and achieve goals you set, and also involves being confident in, and enjoying, your wins. Being self-assured is also a resiliency factor against setbacks. To build your self-confidence and self-efficacy, know your strengths (the second WHAT, see chapter 9) and set goals (the fifth and last WHAT, this chapter).

- *Positive thinking in current situation, and positive thinking about the future:* Important here are a growth mindset, finding the silver lining and turning obstacles into opportunities (the third WHAT, chapter 10).

- *Strong goals:* Goals are what the fifth WHAT and this chapter are all about, and these will give you a clear sense of direction, or a new direction (the fourth WHAT, chapter 11).

- *A motivating environment:* Surrounding yourself with people and resources that will help you move closer to your goals is important in this factor (and I talk about resources and support in chapter 14).

Finding your voice

With self-motivation behind you—and I mean actually literally behind you, supporting you in all your actions—you can find your voice. What do I mean by this? (And I'm certainly not talking about the voices in your head of self-doubt or negative self-talk.)

Finding your voice is about finding something inside of you that allows you to BE you. You develop more freedom to speak up and out, express yourself with confidence, and ensure you are heard. It's about finding your voice and owning it, girl!

Often in male-dominated professions, we can lose our voice or never even let it rear its head. This is another aspect of conforming to the environment, not wanting to be judged for being different (or being a woman), becoming beige. Perhaps we fear we won't live up to our vision, our goals and our dreams and so stay silent.

But don't do this. Don't think this. Instead, remember that what blends in gets forgotten, and what stands out gets remembered.

Celebrating the 'firsts'

This one is a big one for me. The premise behind my Be What You Can't See model is that the era of role models for women in male-dominated professions is not yet over. We are still seeing, reading and hearing every day about some remarkable women who continue to challenge the status quo, break down barriers and take on roles traditionally held by men.

What I find disturbing, however, is that men and women in these professions don't want to make a fuss about these 'firsts' because they want to see it as 'business as usual' or normal. But I say, how can it be 'business as usual' or normal when a woman tackles a 'first'—because women have previously been denied these roles on the basis of sex—and she's the only one. It's not normal.

We need to make a fuss when a woman does this so more women can see that what they did is achievable for them—so more women can be what they *can* see, as well as having to be what they *can't* see. We need to make a fuss so that the men in the organisation understand that the masculine norm is being challenged, that it's time for a new norm.

Just in November this year, Navy appointed its first female Warrant Officer of the Navy (the most senior ranking non-commissioned officer) in the nearly two decades since the position's inception in 1993. Most of the media coverage of this appointment alluded to her significant leadership skills, experience and capability. I know her personally, and there is certainly no doubt of her suitability for the role. Then, very quietly, and without fanfare, the article briefly mentioned she was the first female appointment.

I have mixed feelings about this. Perhaps she didn't want to draw attention to her gender; the 'beige' brigade would argue that she was selected on merit, so what's the big deal?

Well, of course she was selected on merit, but that's not the issue — because again, as I mentioned earlier, we are not quite yet at 'business as usual'.

Celebrating this appointment is more about noting her achievement as a woman, given that Australia was ranked thirty-fifth on the global index measuring gender equality, down from a high point of fifteenth in 2006 (according to 2017 statistics from the Australian Human Rights Commission). More could have been made of her appointment so that other women could see that, despite being a minority in the workplace, they too could aspire to and achieve such greatness.

On a similar note, Navy just announced the name of a seventh division at the RANC at Jervis Bay: McClemens Division, named after Sheila Mary McClemens, CMG, OBE. This is the first time a woman's name has been represented in this way. McClemens (1909–1988) was a lawyer, barrister and company director. She set up the first all-female law firm in Western Australia in the 1930s and was the first female barrister to appear before the Supreme Court of Western Australia.

McClemens joined the WRANS in 1943 and rose to become the Director of the WRANS from 1944, serving until 1947. A notable, accomplished woman and Navy officer, she set up her female practice because she and another woman were unable to find work in a law firm at that time. Perhaps she saw the Navy at that time as another challenge. Who knows? But here is another occasion on which a women's achievement has gone quietly under the radar.

Conversely, in the US in mid-2019, the *New York Times* reported on the first woman to lead a US Army infantry division: Brigadier General Laura Yeager, a decorated helicopter pilot who navigated a narrow path to leadership, and took command of the 40th Infantry Division in the Californian National Guard, a unit that has had men at the helm for more than 100 years.

In the article, Yeager gave thanks to the many officers and non-commissioned officers who had mentored her over the years.

She also said, 'They never once treated me differently because I was female, which is exactly how it should be and how I wanted to be treated.'

And, of course, her success was never about her being female — she would have been selected on merit and, as a senior officer and pilot, had clearly broken that barrier decades before. The point is the US military was celebrating another 'first'.

As the author of the *New York Times* article said, 'Servicewomen like General Yeager are paving avenues for themselves, and for the next generation, as they rise to positions that were once impossible to obtain.' The paper is just pointing out the bleeding obvious; 'first' appointments of women are important because they were appointments in roles previously denied to them.

Yeager herself said, 'I heard someone say a long time ago that "you have to see it to be it". I think there is truth to the idea it is easier to imagine yourself accomplishing a goal when you see someone that looks like you has succeeded.'

The same article also highlighted the appointment of Rear Admiral Shoshana S. Chatfield as the first female president of the US Naval War College at Newport, Rhode Island. Again, another esteemed appointment by a woman for the first time, another celebratory win for women.

On a light-hearted note, I loved the way LEGO, in 2017, decided to celebrate the achievements of women in NASA, based on a submission to the Lego Ideas site by Maia Weinstock, the deputy editor of MIT News. The achievement of the women featured included a few (massive) firsts:

- *Sally Ride, astronaut, physicist, and educator:* A physicist by training, Ride became the first American woman in space in 1983. After retirement, she founded a science educational company with a special focus on girls.

- *Mae Jemison, astronaut, physician, and entrepreneur:* Trained as a medical doctor, Jemison became the first African-American woman in space in 1992. After she retired, Jemison established a company that develops new technologies and encourages students in the sciences.

- *Nancy Grace Roman, astronomer:* One of the first female executives at NASA, and known as the 'mother of Hubble' for her role in planning the Hubble space telescope, Roman also developed NASA's astronomy research program.

- *Margaret Hamilton, computer scientist:* Employed by MIT but working under contract with NASA in the 1960s, Hamilton was the lead software designer for the Apollo missions to the moon, developing the on-board flight software. She is also known for popularising the modern concept of software.

(This limited edition set is no longer available through Lego, but an online search for it still brings up images and details if you'd like to find out more.)

We need to continue to celebrate the 'firsts' for women because they are still unusual, and they are still not 'normal' or 'business as usual'—this can only come with greater gender parity.

I don't think you can argue we have gender equality when we still have the 'first' in something in 2019. And if women have to be what they can't see, we should then actually get to see them!

WHAT YOU CAN'T SEE: HAVING A VISION

One of the most essential elements of great leadership (of yourself and others) is having a vision of what you want and where you want to go.

Irish playwright George Bernard Shaw is often misquoted as saying, 'Life isn't about finding yourself. Life is about creating yourself.' Although no evidence exists that Shaw actually said (or wrote) this, the main point remains.

Yes, life is a creation, and we have the opportunity to create the life we want. But the important question is this: do we often have a clear vision of where we want to go? Can you envision what that created life will look like? Or do you just add to, amend, change or alter your life as you go along?

Most of us just take life as it comes. We're focused on getting through each day. And this is important, of course. But so is thinking about the future in terms of a vision for yourself. Where do you want to be in five years? Ten years? What do you want to be doing?

To get there, to achieve your dream, you have to create the steps. You need to have vision. The word 'vision' comes from the Latin *visionem*, meaning wisdom. Having a vision means having the wisdom to see past certain events in expectation of a greater outcome.

Dr Carmen Harra, a US-based best-selling author and psychologist, suggests that visions become reality as a result of three key factors: creativity, perseverance and actions. Harra also argues that creating a broader vision is the first step to manifesting your ideal life.

And how to do this? Here are some tips:

- Create your B.I.G. (see the following section).

- Take the first step—this might be a massive leap of faith, and involve saying yes even when you don't know how!

- Keep your eye on the ball.

- Be 'Pollyanna'-like or at least find the silver linings in any setbacks along the way.

- Don't be afraid of negativity when it appears—your strengths will help you get through this.

- Don't give up—you have to work to achieve your vision. You've charted a new course, so don't deviate.

- Celebrate the achievements along the way—big or small.

B.I.G. Setting

If building resilience takes and achieves longevity in your industry, then take that long-term view. Having B.I.G.s will encourage you to take up challenges and overturn obstacles and, in the process, build the resilience you need for that long-term view.

I always had a long-term view of my career. Initially I had a goal of twenty years' service because, at that time, our superannuation scheme provided for a pension if you retired after this length of service.

Achieving this security was extremely important to me as a woman and a mother, particularly when I found myself a single mother and primary care giver in the early 2000s when my two daughters were quite young. Financial independence was essential.

I then had a five-year goal to move to Reserve service to give me greater flexibility in work as my oldest daughter started school. Then I had another goal in 2008 when I moved into organisational culture and was presented with an opportunity to take a new direction in my career.

And I've already described where that led in earlier chapters (refer to chapters 8 and 11 in particular).

Another B.I.G. I set was to deploy to Afghanistan, which I did in 2013. This was completely outside the realm of my imagination or possibilities when I was that young officer embarking on my career in 1981.

But the resilience I built in the preceding years set me up, once again, to take on a role no other ADF officer had done, leave my two daughters behind with my ex-husband, and go through the rigorous weapons and pre-deployment training required to keep yourself alive in a war zone. I had to rely on my strengths, values and self-beliefs to manage seven months of isolation, at times fearing for my life, in a strange country.

I faced many challenges, not the least navigating the dangerous streets of Kabul. My first test of resilience was facing a potentially life-threatening situation travelling from my base at the airport to Kabul city. When we travelled outside of the base, we had to wear all our personal protective equipment, including a heavy Kevlar vest with spare ammunition and two weapons to go with it: a 9 mm pistol and semi-automatic F88 Austeyer. And we always had to travel in a two-(armoured) vehicle convoy.

Just as we were passing a small NATO base guarded by Afghan soldiers, we were trapped behind two local vehicles whose occupants were, on the face of it, engaged in a case of road rage. Both drivers had gotten out of their vehicles and were threatening each other with steel pipes.

It seemed like we had been stopped forever (but was more likely only seconds), when my driver, a Canadian Army corporal, said, 'I'll give them thirty seconds more and, if they don't move, we'll just push through.' While we knew this would cause damage to their vehicles, and no doubt create a headache for NATO to address, it was also potentially a car-bomb-suicide situation. Our lives, and those of the Afghan soldiers, were at risk.

But, miraculously, the drivers got back into their cars and moved on. We drove off. Inside I was fighting the terror I had faced, thinking I might not get home to my children. For the first time in my life I was really scared.

Being in that situation, seeing how it could have eventuated into a bomb attack and I could have died that day, really brought home the fact that even if you weren't a soldier fighting the Taliban, any coalition or NATO military person, woman or man, was at risk of being killed just going about their normal duties. And many were.

But the upside of fulfilling this goal was that it gave me many opportunities (as described in chapter 11), showing that they do indeed arise from taking on challenges that stretch you.

I knew it would lead to further work for me on gender and women's roles in conflict; I had set my sights on this niche career path and was on the journey.

My B.I.G., formed when I first became clear about my purpose in 1982, became one of supporting the participation and representation of women in the workplace, particularly in male-dominated professions such as the military, and this continues to this day.

The thing about goals is that they keep your eye on the end game, and on the benefits that come with longevity, commitment and determination.

I've had the adverse experiences I've shared with you that have shaped me, and my career pathways, and given me the resilience to take on challenges, accept knockbacks and move on.

But I've also had a fantastic career:

- I've gained skills, technical qualifications and post-graduate qualifications.

- I've felt the adrenaline in jumping from helicopters, jack staying between ships (a manoeuvre involving moving goods and personnel between moving ships on a jackstay line, and being hauled across by sailors on either side pulling the line inbound), and learning how to handle and fire weapons.

- I've met some amazing people from various non-military organisations.

- I've travelled all over the world.

- I've become a credible national and international expert on gender.

- I've received numerous national awards for my work in advancing gender equality.

- I've become an author.

I've achieved all of these things because I had a vision, set goals, and used the opportunities given to me in my career.

So don't lose sight of the end game that B.I.G. and long-term goals can give you.

Are you ready to set a B.I.G. today?

Ruby McGuire, a Scottish coach, mentor and 'Business Mastery and Mindset Queen', helps women step up as leaders, create a success mindset and master their business. While this is not a book about how to do the latter, it is firmly focused on getting you to step up and create your own success. On her website (www.rubymcguire.com), McGuire says,

> *What I've learned over the years in this long-term game of business is that you need to step up, to be a leader of your business, a Queen. One that takes strategic and brave action, not just any action. One that has clear boundaries and isn't afraid to make tough decisions. One that stands up in front of her people, despite any fears going on underneath. One that ditches the self-doubt, knows her worth and owns it. A Queen that shows up, no matter what.*

Basically, McGuire espouses everything I've been saying throughout this book.

She has created a five-step process to set 'fabulous, meaningful goals', culminating in BIG goals, which I call B.I.G. goals! The following sections, based on McGuire's five-step process, take you through how to set these B.I.G. goals.

Step 1: Start with a mini review

When setting goals, start with the past in mind. Think about what's happened to you in the most recent past and use this to create some exciting new goals.

Action: Consider the following questions. Don't over-analyse your responses to them; this is just a quick review. Write out your answers to the following:

1. What three lessons have you learned in the past six months?

2. What dreams have come true?

3. What three things are you most proud of yourself for?

4. What didn't work for you?

5. What do you need to let go of? (This could be something you didn't achieve.)

6. What would you like to stop, start and continue?

Step 2: Find three little words

In this step, start by focusing on how you want to 'feel'. Write out three words that will help you achieve your goals and bring you the most happiness — for example, freedom, wealth and family, peace, excited and cherished, or organised, positive and fun.

Write out how you already live those words, and then answer the question, 'How would my life/career/role be different if I allowed these three words to be my guide?'

Step 3: Define your three B.I.G.s

This is the time to think really B.I.G. and get excited about your goals.

Complete the following:

1. Remind yourself of your three empowering words from Step 2 and use these to guide your goal setting.

2. Write down what you would REALLY love to achieve.

3. Convert this into three B.I.G.—not just the 'nice to haves', but the ones that excite you from the top of your head to the tips of your toes.

B.I.G. are:

- outcome focused—once you know your WHY, it's easier to be focused on the end game

- in line with your values—the more a goal is aligned with your core values, the easier it will be to achieve

- stated in the positive

- S.M.A.R.T:

  Specific: so you know exactly what you're trying to achieve

  Measurable: so you know when you've achieved it

  Action-oriented: so you can DO something about it

  Realistic: so it IS achievable

  Time-bound: it has a deadline.

Crafting S.M.A.R.T. goals is designed to help you identify if what you want to achieve is realistic and, if so, help you determine a deadline for achieving it. When writing S.M.A.R.T. goals, use concise language but include relevant information. These are designed to help you succeed, so be positive when forming your goals. The following figure provides some questions to help get you started.

Initial goal	What is the goal you have in mind?
Specific	What do you want to accomplish? Who needs to be included? When do you want to do this? Why is this a goal?
Measurable	How can you measure progress and know if you've successfully met your goal?
Achievable	Do you have the skills required to achieve the goal? If not, can you obtain them? What is the motivation for this goal? Is the amount of effort required on par with what the goal will achieve?
Relevant	Why are you setting this goal now? Is it aligned with overall objectives?
Time-bound	What's the deadline and is it realistic?
SMART goal	Review what you have written, and craft a new goal statement based on what the answers to the questions above have revealed.

Another option is to do this exercise using a F.U.N.K.Y. goal-setting system, also created by Maguire. Here's what the letters relate to:

- **F:** Make your goal FABULOUS. It MUST excite you.

- **U:** Create an UNSHAKEABLE plan. Allow time for things that might crop up. Think about aspects such as the times you do your best work.

- **N:** is for NOW. Don't just let the dust settle on your goal and plan. Take one piece of action within the next 24 hours.

- **K:** KEEP at it. Plan to do something every single day towards your goals.

- **Y:** Say YES and commit to success! You can do it, if you just commit and follow through on your plan.

Even though you may be tempted to create lots of goals, don't! No matter what method you use to arrive at your goals, choose only three, no more. When you achieve those three goals you can then move onto setting some more — and keep focused!

Step 4: Review your B.I.G.

Action: Do a check-in to check your goals using the following steps:

1. Ask yourself if these goals are what you REALLY want?

2. Do they get you into that 'WOW' place?

3. Moving forward, what will you BE/DO/HAVE (refer to chapter 7) when you've achieved them?

4. If you could have your goal right now (as in you've achieved it) would you take it?

Step 5: Pull together a three-step action plan for each of your three goals

Now, KISS (keep it simple sailor) and set yourself three simple action steps for each of your three B.I.G.

Action: Write out each big goal and, underneath it, write down three actions to get you started on achieving your goal.

For example, B.I.G. 1: Write a book

Action 1: Book into an author's academy or writing retreat to learn how to approach writing a book. (A good example of this is Andrew Griffith's Author Academy that I attended in Bali in July 2019 and which helped me move past the idea and my procrastination to actually publishing this book, all within twelve months!)

Action 2: Find a good publisher who will help you through the process from start to finish. (Here I do have to mention Michael Hanrahan, a Melbourne-based publisher who gave me the confidence, along with Andrew, to pursue this book.)

Action 3: Start writing, and write every day.

Omne trium perfectum

On a final note, perhaps you're wondering why I have used 'three' throughout this process. As Wikipedia outlines:

> The rule of three is a writing principle that suggests that a trio of events or characters is more humorous, satisfying, or effective than other numbers. The audience of this form of text is also thereby more likely to remember the information conveyed because having three entities combines both brevity and rhythm with having the smallest amount of information to create a pattern … The Latin phrase 'omne trium perfectum' (everything that comes in threes is perfect, or every set of three is complete) conveys the same idea as the rule of three.

Three is used in many ways in Western culture — from in religion (the Holy Trinity), storytelling (*The Three Pigs, Goldilocks and the Three Bears, The Three Musketeers*), literature (the three-act play), or even TV shows (*Location, Location, Location*). Performing actions in sets of three adds strength to the act.

So three seems like a nice, well-rounded number of things to do that will help keep you focused and on track.

Wrap-up

There you have it: five surprisingly effective steps to set your B.I.G. Now you need to do the work — it's time to take action!

MY TOP 5 TIPS

1. Create a vision for who you want to BE, what you need to DO, and what you want to HAVE. Think B.I.G. — brave and important goals!

2. Self-motivation is about the ability to do what needs to be done, without influence or supervision from other people or situations. People with self-motivation and with high levels of resilience can find a reason and strength to complete a task even in the face of adversity or in the absence of any support.

3. The premise behind my Be What You Can't See model is that the era of role models for women in male-dominated professions is not yet over. We are still seeing, reading and hearing every day of some remarkable women who continue to challenge the status quo, break down barriers and take on roles traditionally held by men.

4. We need to continue to celebrate the 'firsts' for women because they are still unusual, and they are still not 'normal' or 'business as usual' — this can only come with greater gender parity.

5. Set B.I.G. and make them S.M.A.R.T!

Part Three

How
TO SAIL
THE SHIP

The pessimist complains about the wind;
the optimist expects it to change;
the realist adjusts the sails.

William Arthur Ward

Thirteen
Walk the talk

She was powerful not because she wasn't scared but because she went on so strongly, despite the fear.

Atticus, from *The Dark between Stars*

So, where to from here? You've done the five WHATs from the Be What You Can't See model, you've charted a new course, you're taking a new direction with your newfound purpose or passion, and you're stepping up and not only taking on the 'firsts' and also celebrating your achievements. You've got this, girl!

Now you have to stand tall, put on your flak jacket and get out there.

You no doubt know what a flak jacket is. And people like me in militaries, police forces or other forms of security services are familiar with using them in conflict zones. Will I incur your wrath by pointing out the irony of women now still wearing flak jackets designed for men, as an example of women having to adapt rather than the system adapting to them? (Hopefully if you have read this far in the book, you no longer subscribe to the notion of 'sameness'—if you ever did!)

The flak jacket is a form of body armour designed to provide protection from case fragments ('frag') from high explosive weaponry, such as anti-aircraft ('flak' is a German contraction for *Fliegerabwehrkanone* or 'aircraft-defence gun'), grenades, some pellets used in shotguns and anti-personal mines and other lower-velocity projectiles. It is not designed to protect against bullets fired from small arms such as rifles or handguns. However, certain flak jackets are able to sustain certain gunshots, depending on the armour, the projectile, the angle at which the shot was fired (an oblique angle, for example), and the range from which the shot was fired.

Of course, you won't expect to see real grenades, pellets, anti-mines or other projectiles in normal life. But they are great metaphors. You'll need the flak jacket to protect yourself from those who seek to demean, diminish or demoralise the new you. You'll need your flak jacket to ward off the pot shots, criticisms, barbs and 'tall poppy' comments from others who are not as brave as you.

When you be what you can't see, you are putting yourself out there. You'll become more public, more well-known. You'll become a keynote speaker, know famous people, maybe even write a book. Then you'll find out who you are and who others are.

Part of my journey to become what I couldn't see was to take my knowledge, experience, training and education to build my profile as a credible gender expert and thought leader. I've shared my thoughts, opinions and comments on social matters having an impact on women and girls around the world on various social media platforms, at conferences and in workshops. And, invariably, anonymous trolls respond online with personal attacks, rather than reasoned, logical and respectful arguments. Only just recently, when I commented on a post on Facebook relating to the level of sex trafficking in the US, and dared to suggest that women were often economic prostitutes rather than choosing a career in the sex industry, one male troll suggested I must have inside knowledge as a sex worker myself. Talk about making it personal!

Over the past few years, I have celebrated various wins or achievements. Some have been national awards, such as the Telstra Business Women's Awards, or the *Australian Financial Review* 100 Women of Influence, twice. I have been published in revered and respected international publications, such as the *Oxford Handbook on Women, Peace and Security*. I have been written about in national newspapers. And sometimes, the silence in response is deafening.

In these times, I often wonder, where is the sisterhood?

I've come to accept this is part of being a 'first', of stepping up and becoming something, becoming someone who has purpose and passion, and someone that seeks to make a difference for others. So, I wear my flak jacket permanently.

But what is important is that I keep going. I keep looking for opportunities, I keep striving to help other women, and I use my journey and how I got here, to demonstrate that you can do it too.

You may stay working in your male-dominated profession, you may move on after this journey. But if you're like me, you'll take this new you, this new direction or course, and use it to your advantage where you are right now.

USE YOUR VOICE

I love the song 'I am woman' written by Australian musicians Helen Reddy and Ray Burton, and performed by Reddy, about strong, independent women. In celebrating female empowerment, the song became an enduring anthem for feminism the world over. Even though it was written nearly forty years ago, its words remain valid for women who find their voice, acknowledge their strength, and want people to know. (No doubt you know the lyrics well, but if not you can find them via a quick search online.)

Now, of course, I'm not advocating that you go around singing the song (well, maybe in the shower). But I do suggest you use your voice with conviction, with authenticity and with intellect, so that people in your workplace can see who you are. This allows you to use your newfound strength, passion, personal brand, values and self-awareness to be that person you believe deserves to be there, to be heard and to be valued.

You can stop being 'beige'.

You can stop being 'one of the boys'.

You can value and showcase your femininity.

You can stand out from the crowd.

You can make being the only or token woman meaningful.

And you can know that what you wear is not as important as the vibes you give off when wearing it.

These are all ways that you can use your voice. Having a voice is your birthright. Your voice lives in your mind, your heart and your soul, and it's the best way to express yourself, verbally, physically and emotionally. Your voice is what has helped you to rediscover yourself through this process. And using your voice is the surest way to build those relationships I talked about in the last chapter, to create connections and live authentically.

Karen Keller, PhD, a US-based women's influence and persuasion expert, claims that women who ignore or lose their voice stumble in achieving their goals, and that this leads to regret. According to Keller, however, the biggest fallout from losing your voice is not paving the way for young women to come. She says, 'Women weren't made to be quiet and sit down,' and she gives eight good reasons for finding your voice[1]. Keller's outlines of these reasons are quoted in the following table.

You can teach me	To be understood	So I can know you	Makes you feel alive
You are the director of your voice. The knowledge in you is valuable and needed by the rest of us.	How does your outer voice match or reflect your inner voice? Being understood is fundamental to your being as a woman.	Your voice is unique, with none other like it. Your voice is a reflection of you. Once you know who you are, share yourself with me.	The first steps in finding your voice may be awkward. In fact, it may be terrifying. It's like searching for buried treasure. Only when you dig do you find gold.
Open new perspectives	**Become part of the conversation**	**Honour your expression**	**To pave the road for our daughters**
Your voice assists in achieving your goals. Finding perspectives that belong to you, are new to you and challenge you are instrumental to your growth.	Use your voice to influence the conversation. Make your opinions heard. The power of your voice is real.	Expression leads to growth. Keeping your voice hidden smothers the beauty inside you. Un-silence yourself.	There is a greater promise for our daughters when we find, open up, and share our voice, and that voice is being heard. Just like our mothers did before us — we pay it forward.

---

1   See http://www.parexcellencemagazine.com/motivation-and-self-improvement/7-reasons-why-women-must-find-their-voice.html for more information.

Choose to find your voice. Fight for it. You'll be glad you did!

THE RULES FOR FINDING YOUR VOICE AND WALKING THE TALK

So, here are my 'rules' for finding your voice and walking the talk — and being what you can't see:

1. *Be the woman who is not afraid to use her voice in the workplace, in meetings, anywhere where it counts:* I remember a woman once telling me that, in meetings, she talked quietly so the men have to strain to hear her. That's one way. The other is to take no prisoners. When a man interrupts, call him out. When he takes your idea, call him out. Stop worrying about the consequences. Recognise the value of your opinion.

2. *Say yes to every opportunity that fits with your purpose, passion, life plan, career or whatever, even if you don't know how to do it:* Be like Richard Branson. You'll work it out later. Trust your experience, knowledge, training, natural instinct and intellect. Have goals, a vision, drive and focus, and be determined.

3. *Celebrate every 'first' for yourself and other women:* Hold them or yourself up as shiny beacons, examples for others to follow. Give other women their 'see it and you can be it' moment if they don't know they 'can be what they can't see'.

4. *Don't hide behind the 'beige' veil:* Be proud of being a woman, acknowledge your differences and the value they bring to the workplace. Don't feel you have to fit in, be 'one of the boys' and in the process devalue yourself. Be true to your authentic self.

5. *Don't worry about others' opinions of the new you:* They're just jealous. Use your emotional intelligence to be respectful and professional, so the only reasons they don't like you is because you are being you. Get out there and own what you do, what you're entitled to and what opportunities you can take.

6. *Support other women:* Support workplace policies and programs that help women move into senior leadership roles,

that give them decision-making responsibilities, and that create more of a critical mass than we are experiencing at the moment. Take the time to learn and educate others on what quotas, targets and merit actually means and how using them properly can make a difference.

7. *Stop being apologetic and don't make excuses:* Florence Nightingale, the founder of modern nursing, once said, 'I attribute my success to this: I never gave or took an excuse.' So true. Your resilience and strengths have gotten you this far. Own your voice, your language, your behaviour. Drop the apologies and qualifiers—stop making statements such as, 'I'm sorry to say this but …' 'I hate to raise this but …'—and others will see you as authoritative and credible.

8. *Accept or take credit for your work where it's due:* Don't minimise your work at the expense of acknowledging others' accomplishments. Not accepting responsibility for the positive role you played won't inspire confidence in your abilities.

9. *Become a power of influence:* Use your influence in a positive way, through building relationships and connections, and identifying solutions, outcomes and results. Influence is purposeful so use it wisely.

10. *Stop wearing the hard hat and put on your flak jacket:* By this I mean, stop knocking your head against brick walls if you're finding your male-dominated workplace too much. Take action on everything you've learnt in this book, put on your imaginary flak jackets (a bit like Superwoman's outfit) and get out there and tackle the issues head on.

MY TOP 5 TIPS

1. Wear your flak jacket every day.

2. Use your voice every day.

3. Follow my ten rules for being what you can't see.

4. Repeat tip number 3.

5. Repeat tip number 4.

Fourteen

Getting support

*One of the greatest values of mentors is the ability
to see ahead what others cannot see and to help them
navigate a course to their destination.*

John C. Maxwell

Now we are really at the stern of the ship. We've charted a new course, and sailed against the wind to be what we can't see. And behind all of this has to be the ways in which you can be supported to keep moving forward. You don't want to drop the anchor now!

MENTORING

One way to get support is to be mentored.

I was never formally mentored in my career. But some men stick out as being willing to help me traverse difficulties in my life, and overcome challenges in my career and work. One is Martin Brooker, a trusted friend and colleague for over thirty-eight years. Martin was a long-time Navy officer, retiring at senior rank and now doing what he does best — executive leadership coaching and keynote speaking.

I first met Martin at RANC in 1981. We continued to cross paths over the years, and at one stage he was my boss. He was always a calming influence, a sounding board and the provider of sage advice. In fact, it was Martin who suggested I consider attending Andrew Griffith's writer's retreat, which I did in July 2019 — and which led to

the writing of this book. It was the end of a long period of procrastination and the beginning of moving forward on this idea I had to
share my journey.

Some other men come to mind, including Trevor Jones, Davyd
Thomas, Mark Binskin, Gus McLachlan and Jody Osterman, all
retired senior military officers I've mentioned previously in my story.
These men also kept the wind behind my sails at one point or another.
I have so much respect for them.

Another particular favourite is Paul Quinn, a retired RN Captain
who was my boss in the early 1990s when we both served at HMAS
Nirimba (an apprentice training establishment) in Sydney. Paul was the
senior logistics officer on exchange from the UK; I was his deputy.
Paul didn't suffer fools gladly, and I saw that often enough. He had
high expectations and demanded professionalism, attention to detail
and duty of care. But he also encouraged initiative, innovation and
difference, and he willingly gave me the space I needed, as his deputy,
to do my job and make sure he did his. He was also funny, inspiring
and clever, and challenged everything he heard or say. He'd often ask,
'Why are we doing that this way?' We became a good match, sound
friends, and even as thick as thieves when it came to having fun in
the workplace. He motivated me to be my best because he trusted me
implicitly. We are still friends to this day.

I've also had some fabulous women friends and colleagues who
from time to time have listened, offered advice, provided guidance. These include some notable high-profile women such as Liz
Broderick, Avril Henry and Maureen Frank, along with some less
well-known but as equally notable senior Navy women, such as
Sandy Coulson, Sue Manning, Carolyn Brand. These women often
provided a soft landing place or a hard edged sword when I needed it!

Perhaps here is not the place to mention Carolyn's kind but firm
guidance to me when I was a young sub-lieutenant, serving at HMAS
Albatross, the Fleet Air Arm base in Nowra, in the early 1980s (but
I will anyway). She wasn't impressed that I was the 'pin-up girl' for
723 Squadron on the occasion of their Wessex helicopters celebrating
21 years of service in the Navy. Enough said here, but I left her office
firmly understanding my very un-female-officer-like behaviour!

A poster girl for Wessex but not a poster girl for women's rights! Still, this was one of the many hiccups along the way I experienced that led me here.

But there weren't many other mentors. Over the course of a very long career, I could count on two hands the number of people who shared my journey and guided me along the way. But what I have learnt over the last few years, particularly from working so closely with women, is that we don't need to have just one mentor, one at a time; we can have more at the same time. I call them the 'board of directors'.

I tell women now, in workshops and when speaking on women's empowerment, to seek out a number of mentors, informal or other-wise, who you can turn to depending on the issue at hand. They can be both women and men.

But I add a word of caution. Just recently, a male friend suggested I should have a senior military *man* write the foreword for this book so that it looked like I'm engaging them in the equality issue. I said, firstly, this is a book for women. And, secondly, why do I need to get a man to validate how women feel? This is almost as bad as another senior male officer I recall suggesting a male colleague of mine deliver a presentation on gender perspective because, as there were more men than women present, they would accept it better coming from a male. I said, 'That kind of defeats the purpose, don't you think?'

In the same vein, don't feel you have to engage men; however, I do think the diversity is valuable, especially if they are gender converts and advocates! In the next section, I talk about the value of empowering men to empower women, only because the reality is that we are working in male-dominated professions. We need to get them on board!

One could be a more senior person in your workplace or field of work (who I call your 'master or mistress of craft'). One could be a senior person who can advocate for you or sponsor you to advance in the workplace (the 'champion of your cause'). Another might be your partner in life (your 'co-pilot') whom you trust and who supports you and your decisions. Someone might be your 'anchor', the person who keeps you grounded, maybe a close friend or family member. And finally, there might be another woman you are mentoring (your 'reverse mentor'). The following figure outlines this 'board of directors'.

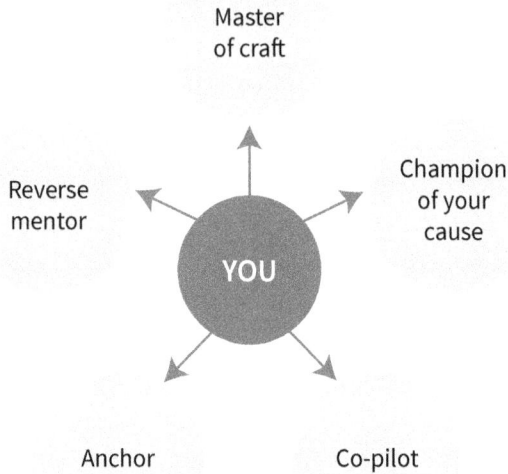

Master
of craft

Reverse
mentor

Champion
of your
cause

YOU

Anchor

Co-pilot

The important point here is to surround yourself with the people who can help you to become what you can't see.

I do think having mentors is an important part of helping you get where you want to go, or who you want to be, but as Diana Ross (American singer and entertainer) says, 'You know, you do need mentors but, in the end, you really just need to believe in yourself.'

EMPOWERING MEN TO EMPOWER WOMEN

Another way to help you navigate your new direction is through empowering men to help you do just that.

I'd like to share a short story with you.

A couple of years ago I had the pleasure of informally mentoring a young male employee of a public service organisation in Canberra, who was then chairing a women's networking forum, and who wanted to stay engaged on the issue of women's equality and empowerment in the workplace, despite avid opposition by women to his chairing role. He was considering stepping down from this role and, in fact, he later did. I was really inspired by his attitude, his actions and his capacity for understanding gender dynamics and its importance to his organisation.

I encouraged him to give some thought to how he could contribute to the discourse on gender equality, and efforts by his organisation to promote and sustain women's participation, especially in leadership roles. I told him he could demonstrate his commitment to this issue in several ways, and continue to support the women he worked with.

Firstly, I suggested he look for ways to work with the women who wanted his chairing role — to act as an adviser, sounding board and in a partnership way. This, of course, would rely on the women seeing him as an essential resource to achieving their goals and outcomes.

Secondly, I suggested that he keep himself informed about all the issues relating to gender equality and share that information in practical ways. This sharing could be through written contributions to the development of workplace policy on equality, as well as ensuring his conduct mirrored the values of equality and equity. I said it was important that he become actively involved in events and forums, within the organisation and externally, and invite other male colleagues to join him, to challenge the thoughts, attitudes and behaviours of his male co-workers who may intentionally or unintentionally perpetuate gender inequality.

Thirdly, I proposed that he look for opportunities to increase the gender balance in teams, forums, networking events, meetings and so on, to maximise the benefits arising from equal representation and gender perspective. This crossed over into a discussion about the impact of gender-neutral policies on both men and women, which in fact could be blind to their different needs and concerns. I stressed the need to understand that equality was not about being the same, but it was about ensuring equal access for men and women and, in doing so, special or temporary measures could be considered to achieve this.

Lastly, I told him to make his effort count. Be that person who is actively involved in workplace relations, policy development and decision-making. Be counted as someone with expertise who can contribute actively in changing the workplace culture to one that values equality for all. Be valued as a male champion who lives gender equality in his own life, at work and at home, who role models equality, fairness and mutual respect.

I caught up with him some time later to find out how he went. Sadly, he felt sidelined and unwanted by the women who had replaced him, and eventually left that workplace. I thought he was a lost opportunity for those women. I don't know what he's up to now because we've lost touch, but I hope he was able to hold true to his beliefs and commitment and make a difference somewhere else.

You can look for the men in your workplace who are willing to support and champion you. You may not be focused on gender issues in your male-dominated workplace per se, but, as a woman, you are a part of those gender issues.

Help yourself, and other women, by finding these champions and supporting and empowering them to support and empower you.

MALE CHAMPIONS

Male allies, advocates and champions—perhaps 'sponsorship' by another name?

It's these men who can become your champion on your 'board of directors'. We often feel we can be over-mentored but under-sponsored, and a champion can be both. Mentoring can only help you get some of the way. But a champion or a sponsor can get you underway!

Some internationally renowned programs are already doing just that.

In 2014, UN Women created a solidarity campaign for the advancement of women, with a goal of engaging men and boys as agents of change by encouraging them to act against negative inequalities faced by women and girls. Men and boys are encouraged to take the HeForShe pledge and commit to being the person who can make the change happen. Thousands of Australian men in workplaces around the country have already taken this pledge.

Then there's Elizabeth Broderick's MCC founded in 2010 and comprising some of Australia's most influential and diverse male chief executives and chairs. The group aims to use their individual and collective influence and commitment to ensure the issue of women's representation in leadership is elevated on the national business agenda. This group includes senior men heading a variety of male-dominated professions such as the military, police, football, mining, investment, politics, judiciary, science and engineering and agriculture, just to name a few.

But even in your own workplace, you can seek out the 'champion' who will make the sailing easier. A boss that ensures you are always given the space to speak up in male-dominated meetings by specifically and directly asking for your input. Someone who understands where you are heading and helps to remove systemic barriers to you reaching a safe port. A person of influence who can role model respectful relationships and call out inappropriate conduct. A senior executive who is prepared to listen to a woman's perspective.

These champions can be women or men and should be both. Often, they are in senior positions and, through their support for you, can affect cultural change in their organisation. This is all that women are after: being valued for who they are, and their gender not being a barrier to achieving their full potential.

MY TOP 5 TIPS

1. Find yourself a mentor or, indeed, many mentors to create your own 'board of directors'.

2. Look for allies and champions — male or female.

3. Empower men to empower women.

4. Reverse mentor another woman.

5. Believe in yourself.

Chart your own course

What would men be without women?
Scarce, sir … mighty scarce.

Mark Twain

It never ceases to amaze me that, even in 2019, men still try to subordinate women. They still make sexist jokes and derogatory remarks, and sexually abuse and murder women, often the ones closest to them. They still make condescending comments about women's looks, capabilities, potential or progress.

In many places, men still control what women wear, what they are to think, their access to resources or even simple freedoms like driving a car. They even seek to regulate women's control over their own bodies, sexual activities and reproductive health. This all happens as much in first world countries as in those still developing.

So, it behoves us all to be the best person we can be to help change that, and it starts with you. An online quote widely attributed to Lao Tzu, an ancient Chinese philosopher and writer, says, 'When I let go of who I am, I become what I might be.'

Today as I write this, I'm finding that 2019 is definitely the year I have become that person I couldn't see. I've transitioned so smoothly from being a Navy officer to an international consultant—almost too good to be true—and have really landed on my feet.

I've started work with UN Women Jordan and preparing for my first mission to Amman in December.

I've just been invited to nominate as chairperson for a new regional security college examining merging security challenges. Separately I've been invited to be a part of a 'brains trust' to develop a Women in National Security conference for 2020.

I've completed my Graduate Certificate in Gender, Peace and Security at Monash University—and (with the advantage of being a long-term practitioner!) have scored High Distinctions on all my assignments. I even amazed myself! I'm very motivated now towards my Master of International Development at the University of Canberra in 2020.

I've completed my Level 1 credentialled practitioner qualification as a coach at The Coaching Institute.

And I finally got around to writing this book.

Add in my two beautiful daughters, their amazing boyfriends, my three cats and newly acquired Labradoodle pup, and I'm living the dream.

You can too.

I was just recently recognised with the Silver Award for 'Most Inspirational Y' at the Gold Coast-based Y Factor Awards. After reflecting on some of the stories I heard from other women over the course of a pre-awards conference and at the awards night itself, all overcoming adversity to achieve so much in their lives, I realised they all have one thing in common. They have all stepped up and not waited for role models to become who they are now. They all made decisions to change the course of their lives and chart a new course—they took command of their career.

Charting your own course starts with recognising who you are and where you have been. It's about knowing upon whose shoulders you stood to get where you are today. I learnt recently that in New Zealand this is known as 'whakapapa', a fundamental principle in Maori culture. A person reciting their whakapapa proclaims their identity, places themselves in a wider context, and links themselves to land and tribal groupings and their 'mana': their power, effectiveness and prestige.

I love this. While I have talked in the book about being who you can't see when no role models exist, this philosophy recognises the role that predecessors play, directly or indirectly, in your path to success. My role is to inspire women to be who they can't see, but I don't necessarily see myself as a role model, or assume they also see me in this way. But I'm happy for them to stand on my shoulders and use their 'whakapapa' to achieve that.

I have always been defined by my military service, in the service of my country and of others. For the majority of my adult life, this has been my tribe (for good and for worse). I only have what I have now—exciting, meaningful and fulfilling work with organisations and people I care about—because of that service. It gave me my why. How effective I am in this work, and the prestige I have earned over the years, come from this tribe, my 'whakapapa' and my 'mana'.

In your journey, find yours.

Secondly, charting your own course means setting sail in that new direction. Taking that newfound energy and doing something with it. So many women I talk to say, 'I'd love to do what you do', and I tell them, 'Well, you can, what is stopping you?' What I have found is that these women still need to go through the steps I've outlined in the preceding chapters to be what they can't see, and only then do they find the courage to step out of their comfort zone and follow their passion, and realise their dreams.

I have a lovely young female Army colleague, Lyndsay Freeman who, now in her early thirties and a mum to two young children, has begun what she calls her 'de-conditioning' from, firstly, what she describes as 'patriarchal values and ingrained gender biases from growing up in a typical Aussie household' and, secondly, what she says she bought into when she first joined the Australian Army. She has finally realised that she can be her true authentic self, she can tap into her femininities and not deny her womanhood, and even celebrate being a woman in a profession that now needs to truly recognise the differences and diversity of genders.

She said to me recently while we caught up for lunch, 'I couldn't stop thinking about your concept of "tacking". I've been obsessing over cementing a career plan but have found some inner peace in the thought that I just need to keep my ship in shape and sails up, ready to seize any opportunity the wind brings!'

She is beginning to be what you can't see!

How relevant is this? Don't deny your dreams. Feed your destiny. You deserve true happiness.

Charting a new course means you might be headed into open seas — and facing excitement mixed with uncertainty, adventure coupled with the unknown. Seasoned sailors insist nothing compares to those exhilarating moments. The bow of the vessel slips out past the breakwaters and takes its first plunge into the wild waves of the wide ocean.

Sounds both wonderful and challenging, doesn't it?

So, *make sure you have set your compass.* Complete all the steps of my Be What You Can't See model.

Stock up on necessary supplies. Make sure you have certainty and belief in yourself as you sail forward, to anchor you to where you are heading.

Assemble your trustworthy crew, your 'board of directors', mentors and coaches. These are the people who will help you sail through rough waters, into calm waters, and into the right port.

A LETTER TO MYSELF

To end the book, I've chosen to include a piece of self-reflection. I was asked this year to write a letter to my 21-year-old self, as part of a 'coffee table' book titled *Postcards from Tomorrow: A Collection of Letters from Inspirational Women to Their 21 Year Old Selves.* This book, to be published in 2020 (and accessible at www.postcardsfromtomorrow. com), will raise funds for Lou's Place, a women's refuge in Sydney.

With the main author's permission, I'm sharing my letter here with you.

My dear girl,

I'm writing this letter as I travel to the Gold Coast to deliver a keynote address at a women's business summit on the trials and tribulations you will face in the coming decades, and also on what you will learn about yourself and others in the process that will hold you in good stead for the years to come. You will one day stand on many podiums as a credible and reputable expert and passionate advocate. So be prepared for the bumpy journey ahead.

Already you have shown resilience and courage in the face of adversity, well before this should have occurred in your young life. True grit! I know you want to make a difference. Continue to be brave, no matter the barriers and obstacles. Don't be afraid to call the system out.

Martin Luther King Jnr said, 'Show me how to take who I am, who I want to be, and what I can do, and use it for a purpose greater than myself.' What you don't know yet is that one day this will be you. You will achieve so much, and you will survive and thrive and become what you couldn't see way back then. You are going to experience some amazing things, many of which will have such a profound impact on you and many women to follow. Being the only woman will often be lonely and difficult, but you will just have to suck it up. In time, there will be more of you.

In following your passion, you will challenge and overcome barriers in your way, you will demonstrate courage and tenacity in everything you do, you will learn from every event, experience and incident, and you will fight for your rights and those of other women. You will become an inspiration and role model to so many women and girls in your journey. You will use this life journey for a greater purpose than yourself.

I am with you every step of the way, holding your hand, guiding you through your successes and failures, creating the pathway—even though you may feel on occasion that it's two steps forward, one step back. As the years go by, you will create a legacy for women that knows no bounds. But be prepared for how long change might take and how hard it will sometimes be.

This will all come at a price. You will face rejection from people who don't understand you, your ideals, your vision or what you stand for. You will experience hostility, intimidation and bullying because some don't appreciate your hard work or efforts. They won't accept or acknowledge the change you will bring. They will feel threatened. But you will also experience love, and the joy of two beautiful daughters who won't disappoint.

Some advice for the hard road ahead:

- *Never apologise for who you are and who you want to be. Embrace every part of yourself, including your strengths and shortcomings and don't look for approval.*

- *Know what you want and ask for it, even if you don't know how. Work it out later. Have goals, a vision, drive and focus, and be determined.*

- *Step out of your comfort zone, have the difficult conversations, don't shy away from difficult or different situations. Use these opportunities to develop your resilience, your mental toughness and your skills, and learn and grow.*

- *Making mistakes is not failure. Failing to learn from your mistakes is failure. Don't waste time with regret. The power to change your own future lies within you.*

- *Don't waste your time with guilt or self-pity or feeling shame if something hasn't worked out right. Find another way but just keep moving forward.*

- *Don't compromise on your values and standards. Maturity is having the wisdom to walk away from people and situations that threaten your peace of mind, self-respect, values, morals or self-worth. Don't limit yourself to achieving what your predecessors did; instead, reach new heights, do what you can't see.*

- *Don't be afraid to say no.*

So, my message out of all of this is even if you don't know where the journey is taking you, step up, be what you can't see, say yes and then work out how, create momentum—and tell people to get the fuck out of your way!

Thank you for sharing this journey with me throughout this book. I hope the stories and insights made you laugh, cry, and everything in between. Most importantly, I hope this book helped you realise that you could be what you can't see!

Thank you.

JW

Acronyms and initialisms

ABS	Australian Bureau of Statistics
ACMC	Australian Civil Military Centre
ADF	Australian Defence Force
ADFA	Australian Defence Force Academy
ADM	Australian Defence Medal
AHRC	Australian Human Rights Commission
B.I.G.	brave and important goals
CDF	Chief of Defence Force
CEO	Chief Executive Officer
HQ	Headquarters
ICU	Intensive Care Unit
KISS	Keep it simple sailor
MCC	Male Champions of Change
NAP	National Action Plan
NATO	North Atlantic Treaty Organisation
NGN	New Generation Navy
NSW	New South Wales
PERMA	Positive emotion, Engagement, Relationships, Meaningful, Achievement
PNG	Papua New Guinea
POTI	Peace Operations Training Institute
RAAF	Royal Australian Air Force
RAN	Royal Australian Navy
RANC	Royal Australian Naval College
RN	Royal Navy

STEM	Science, technology, engineering and mathematics
UK	United Kingdom
UN	United Nations
US	United States
USMC	United States Marine Corps
WPS	Women, Peace and Security
WRANS	Women's Royal Australian Naval Service

www.ingramcontent.com/pod-product-compliance
Lightning Source LLC
Chambersburg PA
CBHW040849210326
41597CB00029B/4782